How to Talk to Your Dog

"Offers insight into animal communication and how people can learn to communicate with and train their pets more effectively."

—*Kirkus Reviews*

"[This book] can teach you quite a bit...resolve mysteries... because her powers of observation are acute and her ethology is solid."

—*Village Voice,* New York City

*   *   *   *   *   *   *

JEAN CRAIGHEAD GEORGE has shared her home with more than one hundred wild animals and dozens of domestic ones. She is fluent in dogese, catish, and birdic; somewhat less proficient in horse talk, and knows a few words in mink, dolphin, seal, and fox. Her long career as nature writer and member of a famous family of naturalists has put her in touch with the foremost animal behaviorists of our day, as well as with scores of ordinary people who, like her, have learned to talk to the animals by living intimately with them. She divides her time between her home in Chappaqua, New York, and a tent in the wilderness.

Jean Craighead George was awarded the Newbery Medal in 1973 for the most distinguished contribution to American literature for children.

How to Talk to Your Dog

Jean Craighead George

Illustrations by the Author

WARNER BOOKS

A Warner Communications Company

This book was formerly published as part of a book entitled
HOW TO TALK TO YOUR ANIMALS.

This book was formerly published as part of a book entitled
HOW TO TALK TO YOUR ANIMALS.

Warner Books Edition
Copyright © 1985 by Jean Craighead George
All rights reserved.

This Warner Books edition is published by arrangement with Harcourt
Brace Jovanovich, Publishers, Orlando, Florida 32887

Warner Books, Inc. 666 Fifth Avenue, New York, NY 10103

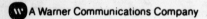 A Warner Communications Company

Printed in the United States of America
First Warner Books Printing: December 1986
10 9 8 7 6 5

Front cover photograph by Saul White

Library of Congress Cataloging-in-Publication Data

George, Jean Craighead, 1919–
    How to talk to your dog.

    Previously published in: How to talk to your
animals. ©1985.
      1. Dogs—Behavior.   2. Human–animal communication.
I. George, Jean Craighead, 1919–   . How to talk to
your animals. II. Title.
SF433.G45 1986   636.7   86-15679
ISBN 0-446-39120-4

To Rebecca Jean Pittinger

Contents

Talkier Than We Knew   1

The Dog   20

Closer Than We Thought   94

How to Talk to Your Dog

Talkier
Than We Knew

A childhood hero of mine was a long-shanked blacksmith with the body of a badger and the eyes of a deer who could talk to the animals. Will Cramer was known as "the man who knows what the animals say." Chickadees clustered around his door; stray dogs came to the gate of his clapboard home as if they had heard through some mysterious grapevine that he would take care of them. Will lived in the valley of the Yellow Breeches Creek in Pennsylvania, down the road from my grandfather's house where my parents, brothers, and I spent our summers. Evenings, my brothers and I often sat on the porch railing of the country store and listened to the farmers talk about crops, the weather, and, now and then, about Will Cramer. "Will listened to a cow bawl today and told Jim Hucklefinger that she wanted to be moved to another stanchion." On another occasion Will heard a dog whine and told his owner, "Your hound wants his collar loosened."

The farmers did not quite believe Will, but did not discredit him either. They were all aware that some kind of communication went on between themselves and their chickens, cows, pigs, horses, cats, and dogs. If it wasn't exactly "talk," it was something akin to it. When the dog barked, they got up and went to see who was approaching the house, and when the cow bawled, they milked her. Communication is, after all, an action by one individual that alters the behavior of another, no matter how humble the creature or how strange the language. A toad excretes a noxious fluid when picked up by bird, beast, or man, that says quite unneatly, "Drop me." Most do.

Will Cramer not only altered his own behavior when the animals spoke to him, he altered theirs by speaking to them in their own language. He asked his dog Nick, who was standing at ease beside him one day, to play by getting down on all fours and spanking the ground with outstretched arms, as dogs do when they are sparking another dog to rough and tumble. He told the cow he wanted her in the meadow by uttering bovine sounds to attract her attention, then stepping in front and walking. In cow language, the animal in the lead is saying, "Follow me."

Anyone watching Will with animals would believe he had some gift not given to other persons, but he told me the year before he died that he just watched what the animals were doing or listened to their vocalizations, then observed what happened next. In other words, Will studied cause and effect, which is how all animal communication functions. A wolf leaves a scent of its presence and social status in its urine at the edge of its territory, and another wolf reads who it is with thoughtful inhalations and either turns away or, recognizing a friend, comes on. "Hello," we say to a person and wait to see the effect of our greeting before going on with the conversation or taking our leave.

Our remarkable communication system—our spoken language, with its infinite combinations of sounds strung together by rules—is so advanced, we believe, compared with nonhuman systems that most of us fail to recognize seemingly simpler dialogues. They are all around us: the cecropia moth calling in chemicals, the spider receiving and sending telegraph messages along a thread, the spreading tail of a peacock speaking of masculinity through a vision of beauty, the wolves keeping their space around them by howling in concert. The odors, poses, movements, displays, and the clicks, hisses, chirps, and bellows are communications. Animals, including us, speak in the four media of scent, touch, sight, and sound. Some messages use but one medium, some all four, but all media, all messages, are the self reaching out to be known by others.

Anyone with even the slightest acquaintance with animals recognizes a kitten's mew as a plea and a dog's bark as a warning. But they are only the tip of the iceberg. Animal communication has turned out to be far more complex than we had guessed until recently.

1920 was a landmark year in our awakening to the true meaning of the prettiest of all animal sounds in nature. That year British businessman Elliot Howard published his discovery that a bird's song is not the outburst of joy we in our innocence had supposed it to be, but a rather businesslike announcement specifically addressed to others of its kind. Birds sing to announce property lines, advertise for a mate, and proclaim ownership of a good habitat for the rearing and feeding of young.

Howard spent years wandering his estate, observing and charting the behavior of resident songbirds. Gradually his notes and diagrams took shape. A certain male bird was always in the same area, he sang from the same bushes and trees, and, no matter how long Howard pressed him, he never left that piece of land. Like himself, the bird had territory, and like himself, he defended it, not with words, laws, and guns, but with song. The seemingly pleasant little bird was threatening his neighbor with, "Keep off my property."

Once Howard recognized this, everyone saw it—and with a deep sense of shock, not so much because birdsong was tough talk, but because it took so many millennia for intelligent mankind to recognize something so obvious.

The discovery of territorial behavior in birds hatched a host of scientific disciplines: ethology, sociobiology, animal behaviorism, cognitive ethology—a potpourri of names for fields in which men and women have put aside the study of conventional physical zoology to observe the thinking, communications, and social behavior of nonhuman animals. Now six decades of their observations have caused a flip-flop in our thinking. We can no longer speak of "dumb" animals. Most natural scientists believe today that the birds and beasts are not automatons, performing by instinct without thought or feeling, but creatures of intelligence and sensitivity that communicate in many ingenious ways. Will Cramer was right: the animals do talk, not only to each other but to us if we listen.

"Talk" and "listen" are impoverished words to use to mean communication; perhaps our reliance on speech explains why we spent so long noticing so little animal palaver. For instance, the oldest, and still most fundamental, medium of communication is chemicals. We are aware of molecule messages as the very few tastes and relatively strong odors we can discern. We consciously use sweets and perfumes in courting. But that's nothing compared with the chemical languages we are not aware of. Every cell of our body is in constant communication through the chemicals called hormones and neurotransmitters. One cell emits molecules of insulin, and another, receiving the word, knows to take up sugar from the bloodstream. Chemical language is most likely all life's mother tongue, for bacteria, from their position on the lowest rung of the phylogenetic ladder, speak in insulin and estrogen. Even plants talk chemically. The alder tree when attacked by insects sends out a chemical vapor that "tells" other nearby alders that insects are attacking. They respond by depleting their leaves of nutrients and loading them with insect-killing toxins. Bacteria speak through chemicals that keep them together where there is food and warmth and bring them together for rare matings.

Scientists are only beginning to unravel chemical communication, but they are sure the lexicon includes the most essential distinction: self and other. Bacteria string along only with their own kind, each joining with others most like itself. On the other hand, a bacterium couples for sexual purposes only with an individual of its own kind that is not identical to itself. The first message might therefore be translated as "I am I," an announcement of species and individual self. Trading such messages, some organisms can apparently gauge their relatedness.

Andy Blaustein, at Oregon State University, recently demonstrated in laboratory tests that pollywogs recognize kin. A pollywog raised separately from its brothers and sisters, and then introduced to them and to unrelated pollywogs of the same species, chose to pal around with its own family.

We ourselves do not seem able to sniff out our degree of kinship, at least we are not aware of it, but apparently we give off a family smell. Nele, a great hairy dog belonging to my friend Sara Stein and very much a part of her family, ran toward a strange man who had parked in the driveway, tasting the air with her nose. Sara was surprised that the dog not only failed to bark at the stranger but bounded up to him in joyful greeting, tail wagging. She looked closer. The man was not a stranger but her cousin, a cousin that Nele had never met but who apparently reeked of relative.

Although our chemical reception is poor compared with a dog's, we do receive and react to some odors, often unconsciously. The smell of a lover lingering on clothes when the lover is away fills us with longing, and the scent of a baby's head elicits tenderness. We no doubt send out odors that announce our sex, but our discernment is nearly subliminal, so we heighten the difference with "feminine" perfume or "masculine" shaving lotion. Few other animals need that hype. Invisible, silent, and unnoticed as these chemicals are to us, our animals easily sniff them out.

A pet red fox I raised had been injured by a man when she was taken from her family den, and ever after she bit or ran from all men. Women she loved, and said so by leaping softly into their lap and draping herself affectionately over their shoulders. It was important to her that she made no mistake, and I soon realized by her reaction of fear even toward objects that men had touched that the red fox could discern maleness and femaleness in the human species far faster and more accurately than I, using my own cultural clues to sex—clothing, voice, and hair. While I often ponder or make mistakes through my eyes and ears, the red fox's nose was instantly correct.

Chemical communication is probably behind dogs' almost eerie ability to read our moods and feelings. While camping with me and my son one summer my son's friend Seaver Jones thought he heard a grizzly bear snapping sticks as it came toward our camp. There was no bear, but Seaver's fear was so great that Jake, his dog, smelled it and raised the hair on his back. Finding nothing himself to fear on the wind, Jake licked Seaver's face and went back to sleep.

Seaver, of course, had no difficulty interpreting Jake's affectionate face lick.

Touch speaks forcefully and intimately, especially among mammals, whose strokes, pats, nibbles, licks, and kisses share a common heritage of motherly love. Mammal mothers and babies literally keep in touch, and so do lovers. But even turtles touch. Last June I watched a male box turtle in my woods approach a female at sundown and after a few surprisingly agile maneuvers for a rock-hard creature, climb upon her back and caress her with loving taps of his lower bony carapace. His touch spoke clearly. She mated with him.

We humans speak of love as we caress, of fear as we cling, of restraint as we grip, and of aggression as we shove. We evoke laughter by tickling. We also send messages to our animals through touch, conveying thoughts that perhaps we do not consciously realize we are saying. The pat on the head we give our animals is a substitute for "Blessings on you, little man," a condescending but reassuring gesture that says, "Remain a child. I'll take care of you."

And our animals speak back to us through touch, although they are not always saying exactly what we think they are. Cats' rubbing and dogs' licking are certainly affectionate statements, but the cat rubs against us to claim us as its beloved possession, and the dog licks us to express its lovingly subordinate position.

I go to the garden to touch talk with a spider, the wizard of tactile communication. I pull very gently on its web; the owner, a female spider, pulls back on the thread. Through her telegraph system she asks, "Who are you?" I could be a male spider or an insect to eat. I pull again, and this time I say with my clumsiness, "Human being." She replies that she knows I am a predator by running up another thread and hiding.

I try other things on her. I shake the web with a slim stalk of grass, hoping to say, "Food," then I sprinkle water to say, "The dew of dawn." I wait for her reply. She does not come out. I toss a katydid in her web, and this time she answers me by dashing out and killing it. I learn her definitions of the insects, for she reacts differently to grasshoppers and gnats, enshrouding each with a defining silk that virtually bears the insect's name. A thick band thrown from a distance is "bee," a broad swath wrapped at close quarters while her feet spin the prey reads "grasshopper," a single thread says "gnat."

To a spider, touch brings messages from a distance along the far-flung web of her communication system. Were a male spider to court her—by drumming his love tattoo from a safe distance before approaching his dangerous bride—she would receive the message in time to avoid harming him. But touch ordinarily requires actual contact, and smell, too, is commonly an intimate communication. The prime long-distance sense in higher land animals is vision. We see and interpret before we encounter. Visual signals, such as a stallion's proud posing on the rim of a distant hill, can be sent over greater distances than animal sound—miles compared to half a mile for the loudest noisemaker, the cicada.

Strangely, until very recently we remained unaware of visual signals of our own more subtle than a wave or a smile. Now, with our knowledge of "body language," we are in a better position to appreciate the expressive faces, poses, and gestures of other animals. Even bodily proportions speak. The proportions of kittens and puppies elicit a parenting response in us, and we say, "Aaaaw," and pick them up. What is talking to us are the large head and eyes, the small body, and short, plump limbs. "I am cute. I am helpless, hold me, care for me," the baby proportions cry out. We are not taught the message of proportions; it comes from deep in our nonintellectual being, down with loving and needing.

Our animals also reply to babyish proportions with parental behavior, even when the baby is another species. Our bluetick hound, Delilah, had such a response to my son Luke when he was a baby. She licked and encircled him and leaped into his crib to curl warmly beside him when I was in another room. She did not do this to Luke's six-year-old sister or four-year-old brother or to me. That's baby power for you.

Adults display their power by posture, and these visual signals, too, are well-nigh universal. The signal is given by making oneself appear big. The wolf says "I am leader of the pack" by holding his head higher than the others. The gull chief throws out his chest and stretches his neck above his kin to announce his dominance. The male songbird puffs up his feathers to speak of his importance and aggressiveness. Kings, queens, and presidents are taught to carry themselves erect. Military officers thrust out their chests like pigeons to say the same thing—"I am dominant and powerful."

The opposite message—one that indicates a low position on the social ladder or an acknowledgment of inferiority in an encounter—is given by making oneself appear small or childlike. The wolf and dog roll over puppylike on their backs in deference, the low-order gull pulls in its neck and crouches, and the humble servant bows to royalty. These postures are extremes and therefore are easy to recognize.

But there are as well an infinite number of other communicative poses, including those of the face, that amplify, dampen, and even contradict "outspoken" messages. Many of our facial expressions—from smiles to frowns—are congruent with what we are saying: when a dear friend says, "I am so happy to see you," the broad smile amplifies the spoken message. We are aware that this is not always so. Even children pick up an insincere smile, despite its being coupled with the words "What an adorable child!" By filming people in stressful situations, such as getting fired, psychologists in California have compiled a "dictionary" of facial messages that contradict spoken statements. Written on these faces are such messages as "masked anger," "overly polite," and "resigned compliance." Facial expressions speak truer than words.

Few other animals have such well-developed—or even as many—facial muscles as we, so a horse's or cat's face seems rather blank to us. To understand what they are saying, we have to learn to read ears, whiskers, the pupils of the eye, and the glint of teeth. They, too, can modify a voiced message. A dog growling with ears pricked is quite sincere in its threat to bite. A dog growling with ears lowered is as frightened as it is annoyed.

Light is another form of visual communication in the nonhuman world, and none uses it so beautifully as the firefly. I grew up in firefly country. When I asked my grandfather why they had lights, he answered, "Because lights are lovely. That's reason enough," and I accepted that. In the late 1950s a persistent firefly observer discovered something that changed the summer night for me. "The lights are a language," he told me one evening. "A simple code. When flashed, the signal is 'Yes'; when off, it means 'No.'" He pointed to the lights above the meadow.

"The fireflies that are blinking and climbing upward are males advertising their sex, which species they are, and their sexual readiness to the females in the grass."

Now as I walk along a stream at dusk, I see loveliness and much more. I see the drama of firefly love. A male glows at the top of an ironweed, lifts his hard outer wings, vibrates his gossamer underwings, and takes off. He climbs, flashing his lamp at a leisurely beat as he courts the females first with slow strokes, then faster and faster. They watch from below. When he reaches the tops of the trees, his call comes even more urgently; the night is passing. A female at the base of a clump of foxtail grass is finally aroused. Her light goes on— "Yes." The male fastens his many-faceted eyes on her and descends. He, too, is ready. His light says, "Yes."

The lamp in the grass goes out—"No." Did another male find her and turn off her light? The downward-gliding male still flashes his bold visual cries and is answered by another light in the grass. He descends, flying past a male who at that instant is caught by a bat, nipped, and crushed with his light on. He falls, his continuous glow becoming a statement of death. It is not a communication, for no firefly upon seeing it changes its behavior. All continue to shine and signal. The glowing body falls to earth like a star and goes out. "No."

The male I am watching drifts into the meadow grass. The "No" female of the foxtail lights up again—"Yes." He touches down on her grass blade.

Both lights go out. The firefly embrace is invisible to bat, frog, skunk, and me, and a conversation in lights is over.

As lovely as this conversation is, to most people the ultimate in visual communication is the peacock. Every pattern and color, from the iridescent head, chest, neck, and golden coverts to the spreading tail and wings, says, "Choose me. I'm beautiful." The peacock's beauty is a result of what is called sexual selection. The peahens have created this wondrous creature over the eons by selecting the most beautiful male to be father of their offspring. And because of their eye, we have among us the super star of visual talk.

Honeybees employ dance to communicate visually with their sisters. Sociobiologist Edward O. Wilson compares their language to our own because they can, like us, speak in symbols. Through a dance one bee passes on to another information removed in time and space.

A forager bee returning to the hive after finding a good source of nectar and pollen alights on a hive wall and runs a figure eight until she gathers her sisters around her. As she dances she puts the emphasis on the *straight-line run* down the middle of the figure by vibrating her body. Were she dancing on a flat surface, the straight-line run would point directly to the flowers. But the hive wall is vertical, so the bee, in effect, pins the map up on the wall. Just as we might use the compass points to describe direction—twenty degrees east of north—she uses the present position of the sun—twenty degrees to the right of the sun. But the hive is dark, so, by convention, she uses "up" to indicate the sun's position. We use a similar convention: north is "up" on our maps.

The distance to the flowers is calculated and translated into time. In one species of honeybee, a run of one second duration indicates the food is five hundred meters away. A two-second run states that the nectar is two kilometers from the hive. During the dance the sister bees call upon other communication systems. They touch the dancer to discern the vigor of her waggling, an indication of how promising she considers her find. The smell and taste of the pollen and nectar on the dancer tell them what flowers they will be looking for. Once briefed, they take off; and the majority arrive dead on target—which I couldn't do by following verbal directions.

Communications so unlike our own as the bee's dance have taken researchers untold hours of observation and experiment to decipher. They are not languages that Will Cramer, blessed as he was with intuition, could have translated. He, like most of us, was more at home with sounds.

As an admirer of animal sonance, I seek out, in the early summer, the most famous theater for croaks, growls, squawks, songs, trills, pipes, and whistles—the swamp. Up from the water surface, out of the reeds, and over the floating plants soars the full choir of animal voices. Insects, amphibians, reptiles, birds, and mammals speak with such volume that I am tempted to add a human song to the glorious clangor. One spring night while camping in the Okefenokee Swamp of Georgia, I heard between sundown and sunup barred owls hooting, alligators bellowing, a wildcat caterwauling, raccoons growling, twenty-two species of frogs piping, and several hundred species of insects buzzing, clicking, whining, and humming. In the dawn light, the shriek of the wood ibis, the carol of the vireo, the rasp of the pileated woodpecker were added, one voice upon another, hundreds of species strong. It was a night and dawn of expressive doings, and my great pleasure was that I could translate a few of their phrases because of the new knowledge in animal communications.

That new knowledge is, however, minuscule. We are on one side of a great abyss that separates human from animal language, and the distance often seems uncrossable. How can we really know what is going through a dog's mind when it wags its tail? We can never get inside its brain. But we cannot get inside each other's minds either. How do I know you see the color green as I see green? What is important is that the dog sees something and is wagging its tail. What it is that makes the dog happy is where we should be looking. As it happens, dogs wag their tails only to living objects—butterflies or people—but never to anything inanimate or dead, not even to a bone. That says something about dogs, even if we can't come up with an exact translation for what they are trying to convey to a butterfly. There is a why to smell, touch, sight, and sound signals, and the why is to be found, as Will Cramer saw, in what happens next. When dogs wag their tails to one another, they then approach in a friendly manner.

So we know that friendliness spells happiness to dogs. Perhaps they invite butterflies to play across an abyss much greater than the one that separates our two mammalian species— one that never will be bridged.

When I read who on this earth was the first speaker to have organs specifically designed to make noise, I felt as if someone had thrown a rope across even that impossible abyss for me. The first voice was so simple and so sensible. It was uttered by an insect, a grasshopper, a fragment of which lies trapped in a fossil 200 million years old. The grasshopper had sound-making files on its wings almost like those of the modern grasshopper. Back in that mist of time, the file owner rubbed his wings together and vibrated the air. The ripple reached a receptor on another of his kind, and she followed the sound to its source. They mated. The first noisemaker needed never again to waste time and energy running around looking for a mate.

To become aware of the languages other species speak is thrilling, but to exchange conversations in these lexicons with another species is the quintessential effort. We all wish we could hold a discourse with our animals, if only to know how they like us. A few people manage to communicate across the abyss with little effort: the rare Will Cramers, a handful of scientists. But there are universal messages that wing across the gap when we least expect it. My brother, John, had a pet coyote named Crooner many years ago in Wyoming. The pup moved on the fringes of John's family life but was never really a part of it. He would come in to play, request food and affection from time to time, and then vanish into his own world in the sagebrush. One day while John was nailing shingles on the roof of his house, he saw his two-year-old son tumble into the irrigation ditch. He still does not know if he yelled or simply scrambled frantically to get off the roof, but the coyote received a distress message from him, appeared like a white knight, and pulled Derek out of the water.

"Danger to the young," he must have conveyed, and the coyote understood it.

Will Cramer never opened a book on animal behavior or took a course in dog obedience, yet he talked to the animals, according to his own analysis, by listening for those expressions we all have in common and conversing on those subjects.

One day I asked Will to tell me how I could let his cat know I wanted to be her friend. He demonstrated by making soft squeaky noises with his lips and holding out his hand. I made soft squeaky noises and held out my hand—and was swatted.

"Too much eye," Will said. "To ask a cat to be a friend, you have to mostly look away." Then he added, "Besides, you smell wrong. The cat smells that you think people are the only critters who can talk."

And he was right. An inside voice from my background in a scientific family was pulling, saying, "Don't anthropomorphize. Don't attribute human thoughts and emotions to animals."

Years later, after raising 173 wild and 50 domestic pets, I still felt that pull, although I had learned to peep like a quail and make hand signals to our mink to invite her to leap and tumble on the back of the couch. Despite such enormous triumphs, my human viewpoint prevailed—only people can truly converse.

It was not until I read a scientific paper on the language of the wolves by the esteemed animal behaviorist Rudolf Schenkel of Switzerland that I believed there were other languages and perfectly brilliant conversations going on on the other side of the abyss. Wolves talk among themselves, Schenkel observed, with eyes, postures, scents, body contact, mood, and voice. And we can use the same signals to talk to wolves.

A few phone calls to wolf enthusiasts informed me that wolf talk and human talk was being exchanged at the Naval Arctic Research Lab in Barrow, Alaska, on the North Slope where the Arctic Ocean laps the land. I approached a national magazine, took on the assignment to "talk to a wolf," packed up, and flew with my youngest son, Luke, to the Top of the World. In that Arctic wildland I interviewed the authorities on wolf behavior and observed the wolves for many long twenty-four-hours-of-daylight days, listening for the only thing I understood at the time—the sounds of whimpers, howls, sniffs, and barks. After practicing the sounds, I felt I was ready to make the crossing of the abyss. I selected a beautiful female I called Silver. She was almost white, her eyes were gold and serene, her disposition, despite her confinement in a large enclosure, was sweet. In broken wolfese, I whimpered my affection and asked her to be my friend.

She ignored me.

"Your pose is wrong," wolf-language expert Dr. Michael Fox said. "Say it with your body." I stood more confidently and moved with more dignity. Still no response. Fox assumed a kingly attitude. I copied his posture and lifted my head with authority, but my whimpers and poses still brought no response from Silver. I was not getting through. There was no change in her behavior. She walked past me as if I were less than a pebble on the tundra.

The day before I was to leave Barrow, I went back to my notes and read something I had skimmed over. The wolf father leads the pack on the hunt, the mother attends to the pups, and baby-sitters and the puppies mock fight, tumble, and play games. The wolf family is very much like the human family; within it conflicts arise and arguments are settled, jobs are assigned and done.

A feeling of similarity replaced my feeling of strangeness. Silver and I had much in common. We were both parents, females; we both watched and disciplined our young, taught them safety rules, encouraged their play, and stopped their aggressions. We had common ground on which to meet and talk. I put away my notebook and went back to the animal lab.

When I approached Silver's enclosure on this last visit and whimpered to her, she hesitated and . . . passed me by.

But as I turned to leave, Silver stopped in her tracks, then galloped back to me. She smiled. Wolves pull back their lips and smile just as we pull back our lips and smile, and for the same reasons. They are pleased, or they like you.

With that smile she let me in. I was not a pebble on the tundra. I was in her consciousness. Having admitted me, she continued the conversation. She wagged her tail, looked me in the eye, and whimpered in a high thin voice, "Uummum," the wolf plea for friendship.

I whimpered, "Uummum." Silver wagged her tail enthusiastically, spanked the ground with her forepaws, and asked me to play. I, at long last, was talking to a wolf.

I did not do anything differently that last meeting with Silver, but I felt differently. I had drawn on our likenesses, not our differences, and, in doing so, I had come down from the pedestal that human beings put themselves on. As Will Cramer might have said, I "smelled right."

The conversations that await us as we learn to reach across the abyss are no doubt full of surprises. One man, Dr. George Archibald, founder of the International Crane Foundation, Baraboo, Wisconsin, must know this better than anyone. He heads an institution dedicated to saving from extinction the stately cranes, among them the whooping crane. Archibald has studied crane communications and their behavior so thoroughly that he can not only share the universal meeting ground with them but *really* talk and get them to answer.

A female whooping crane named Tex, one of the last 150, was given to Archibald by the San Diego Zoo. The bird was imprinted on people; that is, she had been raised from an egg by humans, and she thought she was human, too. When she matured, she fell in love with Archibald.

At five years, when she was of breeding age, she would not mate with her own kind for love of Archibald, and so she was artificially inseminated.

It did not take. Tex was unable to ovulate without the stimulation of courtship. But she, like others raised in captivity, would not tolerate the attention of a bird of her species.

Archibald saw a possibility in his relationship with Tex and decided to try his luck.

He would walk slowly into her outdoor enclosure and begin to speak to her of love in her own language. When she flapped her wings—the equivalent of a wink from a lady in our own body language—he would flap his preposterous and awkward arms. As clumsy as this suitor was, she encouraged him because she loved him and he was talking crane talk. She would float into the air and drop back to earth. He would jump and come down. He would utter strange cries in response to hers and spend as much time as he could spare walking and waltzing with Tex. She was inseminated and laid an egg. But the egg was not fertile. Tex had not reached the climax of crane courtship, and without achieving this, her eggs could not be fertilized.

The following breeding season Archibald took time off from his travels and duties and devoted the day to Tex from sunrise to sunset. They met in the morning and flapped arms and wings. They leaped lightly over the grass and jumped into the air, Archibald stretching his neck in imitation of Tex's stretch. They walked together, gathered worms together, and finally built a nest of grass and corncobs together. One morning when Tex danced with more excitement than Archibald had seen before, she was artificially inseminated. It took. A fertile egg was laid on May 3, 1982. The whooping crane Gee Whizz was hatched on June 3.

In the following chapters you will learn the history, social behavior, and language of dogs—animals that touch our lives very closely.

"Animal talk is on the other side of words," Will Cramer once told me as he explained his uncanny communication with his dog Nick. "He watches my eyes to know what I am thinking; I watch his." But Archibald could not have courted a crane without studying its biology and learning the meanings of its whoops, leaps, and flaps.

So on the one hand, my guide will be the intuition of pet owners who, by their experience, just know how to talk to animals, without knowing exactly how or why what they do works.

On the other hand, my guide will be the scientists who have unraveled a few of the mysterious threads of animal communication through careful and objective research.

For those who need more than Will Cramer and the scientists to make them believe that they, too, can cross the abyss, may I say that if alder trees can communicate with alder trees, why not dogs with dogs, and cats with cats?

And for those who accept this but doubt that cats can talk to people and people to cats, let me mention that creosote bushes can communicate with weed and flower seeds in the soil beneath them—and tell them chemically not to grow.

When I learned that, I went out and talked to everything.

The Dog

Classes were over for the day at the University of Alaska in Fairbanks, and Steve Wood hurried down the corridor of the zoology lab to meet and walk home with Orion, his malamute. The dog, who was curled in the snow near the entrance to the building, heard Steve's footsteps among the many, got to his feet, and waited for him at the door. When Steve appeared, Orion pulled back his lips in a dog smile, and his curly tail beat over his back like a metronome.

"Come on, fellow," Steve called, and Orion swept toward him like an onrushing avalanche. His head was slightly lowered, ears down and back. The lower lids of his eyes lifted, softening his facial expression. His tail wagged his whole rear end joyously. He sniffed his master.

"Hello," Orion was saying in dog talk.

Steve dropped to his knee, took the dog's head in his hands, and shook it affectionately. The movement was of father to son.

"Hey, Orion, how's the boy?"

Orion took a deep draft of Steve's odor and licked him under the chin to tell him he was a person of great status. Steve replied by patting his head, a friendly way of agreeing with the dog's perception of his rank. Orion lowered himself onto his belly and uncurled his magnificent tail in deference. Having made that statement, he arose and barked to bind them together after their long separation and to announce himself to Steve in a more individualistic way—"It's me. Take notice."

Steve hugged the furry malamute and looked into his eyes. Orion gazed back, and after a moment they started off across the campus, the man grinning, the dog wagging his tail—two expressions that mean the same thing.

On the way home the malamute spoke to his master again. The message made no sense to Steve, and for a few dangerous moments he did not understand its purpose.

"We started down the road side by side, walking along quietly as we do," Steve recounted to me several months later. "It was getting dark, so I stuck up my thumb to hitch a ride. A young kid driving a sports car pulled up and stopped. When I made a move to open the door, he spun the wheels and took off, rubber burning, stones flying. He disappeared in smoke. I shrugged—'The kid's nutty'—and walked on.

"A short way down the road, Orion leaped on my chest with his front feet. That's taking over in dog talk, a way of telling me he was boss. But he had never said that to me before. He barked, dropped to the ground, and jumped on me again. He's strong, and I staggered backwards.

" 'Are you crazy, too?' I shouted. 'What's the matter with you?' I yelled at him again, and, with that, he threw all his weight against me. I fell into the snowbank. It was then I saw the sports car coming down the road wide open, headed right at the spot I had been a second before."

TWO OF A KIND

That there is communication between dog and man no owner will deny, but how to read it is not always clear. Dog owners the world over perform the ritual greeting Steve and Orion exchanged every day, aware of the mutual happiness it expresses but perhaps not aware that they have also discussed rank, relationship, obligation, and individuality. Steve Wood's perceptions had been sharpened by his years of studying biology, but even he was surprised at the rescue.

"Apparently Orion had sensed something crazy about that kid," Steve said. "And when he heard the car turn around and start back, far beyond my hearing range, he became my boss and ordered me off the road. He saved my life. I'm convinced of that."

We have poor senses of smell and hearing compared with dogs, and their communications among their own kind depend largely on both. Our precisely muscled faces show emotions more dramatically than dogs' faces, and so we sometimes fail to notice their subtler expressions. Lacking a tail language ourselves, we see only the "loudest" tail words and miss the softly spoken statements.

Nevertheless, the two species have much in common. Dogs and people both speak about rank, territory, and relationship. To both, most communication is in the service of maintaining social order and the individual affections that glue the group together. To discuss these things with dogs, it is important to know their social structure and how they converse about it among themselves. Dogs talk to dogs the same way dogs talk to us. Once you know what they are saying, you can talk back to them.

The ancestors of the dog were wolves who, like early humans, had specialized as big-game hunters. In fact, wolves specialized much more than we did. The whole canid, or dog, family has a short digestive tract that can't handle much in the way of vegetables. In the wild, canids are obliged to live on meat. Although any wolf can catch a rabbit—and it will even stoop to rodents if it must—its favorite food is the large herd animals also preyed upon by humans. We and they have been, and we now are, the most important predators of hoofed animals, such as deer, elk, and caribou. These large and swift animals can outrun both a single man and a single wolf and can kill with the strike of a hatchet-sharp hoof or gore with an antler. Only the large cats, which leap on the back of their prey from ambush and hang on with their claws, can dispatch a deer without help. Wolves have evolved to hunt with their kind, as have humans.

Cooperative hunting means that individuals coordinate their actions, each one communicating its intentions, so that all the others can figure out what they must do to get the job done. Wolves and people evolved a system of coordination that relies heavily on a leader who, as we so often hear, must have "fearlessness," "initiative," "good communication skills," and that mixture of aloof discipline and reassuring goodwill we might lump together as "management ability."

The boss wolf is called the *alpha* wolf. He (more rarely she) decides which animal to pursue, orders the attack, or calls off a futile chase. He chooses which portion of their perhaps ten-square-mile territory to "camp" in temporarily, and he leads the pack to a more promising area when that one has been depleted of game. The leader is respected, indeed loved, by his pack. They look to him for guidance when the crack of a twig might mean danger. They turn to him when a raven calls an alarm or an unfamiliar scent is on the wind. They are like children looking to a parent for reaction and guidance.

There is also an alpha female who dominates the pups

and other females and who is the mate of the alpha male. On rare occasions a female will be the leader of the pack, probably because she outranked the male next in line for the job when the alpha was killed or died of old age.

Second in the hierarchy is the vice-president, or *beta*, the alpha's best friend and the animal who takes the lead when the alpha tires, who assists him and instantly responds to his wishes, and who is relied on to initiate some activities on his own. Every wolf in a pack that may number from two to more than twenty has a specific place in the hierarchy, each labeled by biologists in the order of the letters of the Greek alphabet.

The hierarchy serves both business and pleasure. It erases the uncertainty that an individual might feel if it did not know how to behave or how others would respond to its behavior. In a wolf pack, social relations are as benign as in those finely tuned human families in which each member is reassured by the reliable behavior of all the others. And, as in such a family, each member has a job to do. One may guard, another scout or track, chase, ambush, or attack. These roles are less strictly defined by social position than by talent. The alpha couple, for instance, is always prominent in the hunt, but allowances are made for age, sex, health, and other circumstances, so an individual's job may change from one hunt to another and over its lifetime. On the other hand, an individual with an unusually good nose will probably be sent out for as long as it lives to scout the odors.

SPEAKING OF STATUS

Social position can change among wolves as it does among humans. This is something a dog owner may notice when he introduces a brash young dog into a family in which there is also an aging pet. The young one may challenge the older dog's position—chase it from its food, take over its favorite sleeping spot, push for more affection—and then the old dog's status falls. The dog is noticeably depressed: head and tail droop, the ears are held low. Like the old family dog, an older wolf may give up his position. An aged alpha in Mount McKinley National Park walked off and left his pack when challenged by a younger leader. A "lone wolf," he roamed the forest living off small game until he died several months later.

This is the permanent posture of the wolf who is at the bottom of the ladder. He or she is called the *omega* (Z) and is the weakest member of the group, the one who defers to all others. The omega is, however, an important part of the group, for that individual defines the bottom of the social hierarchy.

With each individual settled into place, from alpha to omega, peace reigns in the wolf society and the animals can work together to the benefit of all. The only time a wolf pack is disrupted is when the boss weakens or dies. Then there is a scramble for the top, and individuals behave aggressively or fearfully until order is restored within a new hierarchy.

With the evolution of the cooperative hunting society, a complex communications system developed that includes giving orders, disciplining, expressing affection, and pulling rank to get work done. Much wolf talk is about rank, each one announcing its position in scent, poses, and facial expressions or replying to the assertions of others.

The leader of the wolf pack speaks of his rank by holding his head and tail higher than the others. If any doubt his position or violate his rules, such as trying to mate when there are too many in the pack for the number of prey animals, he stands over them. They respond to his posturing by lowering

Omega greets alpha

themselves before him, by crouching, or by drooping heads and tails. Once his dominance is established, he need only glance at a wolf that is getting out of hand to get it to cooperate.

Because people use similar signals among themselves, dog owners intuitively raise up to tower over their dog when it is behaving badly and stare to warn it away from the pretzels on the coffee table. These messages work because, to a dog, its master is its alpha. One of the great pleasures of having a dog is, in fact, that no matter what our status is among other people, we are Number One to our pet.

The glue of a cooperative society is friendliness and respect for one another. Wolf friendliness is expressed in smiles—not the broad grin that humans are capable of, but a slight opening of the mouth and pulling back of the lips at the corners (some dogs expose the teeth like people)—and in smoothed foreheads, wagging tails, licking, and mouthing. Respect is expressed by an acceptance of the less talented

Dog greets master

individuals. The lowly are not abused unless food is scarce and the lives of the pups are threatened.

Friendliness and respect within the pack are in contrast to how a wolf feels about strangers. They are simply not allowed in the pack's territory; if a stranger doesn't leave promptly when chased, it will be attacked. A stranger can gain entry into the pack only when numbers are low and another pair of eyes and ears and four legs are needed. Strangers may also be admitted to a pack; they bring in a fresh genetic strain. Usually pack members are related to one another and have known each other from birth. They are a family.

This, too, is something dog owners respond to intuitively. We give a dog a "place" within our family—a bed and a bowl—and we expect it to respect and love all family members, regardless of their size, strength, or personality. You'd probably feel hurt if your dog took to strangers indiscriminately. Many people keep a dog expressly to keep their family safe from strangers.

Because wolves share with us an alpha social structure and strong family ties, and because they are even better hunters than we with their keen ears and noses, it is natural that they were the first animals to be domesticated. The oldest fossil remains of dogs have been found in the Yukon and have been carbon-dated at twenty thousand years, many millennia before chickens and sheep were brought under our stewardship. Dogs live today in closer association with man than any other beast.

Zoologists in general agree that the dog, *Canis familiaris*, is descended from tamed wolves. Taming a wolf pup is not difficult, and it is still done by canid experts, Eskimos and Aleuts. Since dogs can also breed with other close relatives—including the dingo, coyote, and jackal—the numerous breeds and mixes of dogs we have today may represent a delicatessen of canid genes. But whether you have a Pekinese, whose origins are lost in time, or a malamute, which until only decades ago was bred back to wolves to improve the stock, conversations with your pet are mostly in wolfese, and to its human alpha and family the dog brings all the love and respect the wolf gives its leader and its tribe.

Also, although domestic dogs by now have acquired, through selective breeding, a wide range of sizes and shapes—from the Irish wolfhound that stands three feet high at the shoulder to the six-inch Chihuahua and from the short-legged dachshund to the blockbuster bulldog—all behave as though they were among us to hunt.

The forty million dogs in the United States are mostly household pets, but their heritage as hunters dominates their behavior. The dachshund with its short legs will dig and go into a hole given its druthers. The English sheepdog herds its human family if it does not have sheep, using the same strategies a wolf might use to run a herd of caribou. The hound, given a run in the woods, tracks rabbits, raccoons, or—most exciting of all and a wolf favorite, too—deer. The pointer will freeze behind a city window and point the pigeons on the sill, and the Labrador with no birds to retrieve brings back rocks and shoes. Playful as these antics may seem, they are all part of the hunting repertoire of wolves at work.

WILD CONVERSATIONS

Animal behaviorists are gaining insight into the language of the canids by studying their natural behavior in the wild or under semiwild conditions, such as those where wolf packs are enclosed within a territory two or three acres in area. Interested in learning dogs' mother tongue and fortified with background material from zoologists and animal psychologists, I journeyed to the Naval Arctic Research Lab at Barrow, Alaska, to observe semiwild wolves, a pack of seven in a quarter-acre enclosure. There Dr. Edward Folk, a physiologist with the University of Iowa, was studying the heart rates of an alpha and omega as they confronted each other alone and then within the pack. Results? When the alpha and omega faced each other alone, the alpha's heart rate was low, the omega's racing. When returned to the pack, the alpha's went up, the omega's went down as he slunk off to his low but comfortable position in the pack.

While in Barrow I learned that Dr. Gordon Haber, then a graduate student, was gathering data on the wolves of Sanctuary River in Mount McKinley National Park as a follow-up on Adolph Murie's famous study "The Wolves of Mount McKinley." Through bush pilot, radio, and word of mouth I contacted Haber; and through word of mouth, radio, and bush pilot came back the invitation to visit him. I joined him three days later.

The pack consisted of a gorgeous black alpha, his vice-president (the beta), the alpha female, the omega, and nine four-month-old pups. I watched them from a distance through a spotting scope, for wolves are man shy. At first, it was hard to pick up even the gist of a conversation, much less the nuances, but by the end of ten days' spying through the spotting scope, I could compile a typical night's communications.

They slept off and on all day. Twilight does not come to the sub-Arctic in midsummer until 11:30 P.M. In the bright six–P.M. light one evening in late July they got to their feet, yawning and stretching and glancing at the alpha to see what he was doing. The pups got up. Some had slept in shallow saucers scratched into the tundra and others in the summer den, a tunnel in the ground where they also hid when frightened. When the pups were three months old, the pack had moved to this summer camp from the whelping den, or nursery, three miles away on a high ridge that overlooked a river valley where moose and caribou lived or trekked. The present camp was out on the gray-green alpine tundra under snow-covered peaks, far from grizzly bear territory.

For the next half hour the wolves conducted a ceremony that would seem vaguely familiar to anyone who, after spending a quiet Sunday reading the paper or watching a ball game, gets up and arouses his dog to the expectation of an outing. The ceremony started quietly and built in excitement. First, the alpha female walked up to her mate and leader. He sniffed her nose, then she sniffed his. They wagged tails and stood head to tail. The alpha smelled the female's genitals briefly, just enough to check on her state of health, his "How are you?" to her. She brushed against him, and he enclosed her muzzle in his mouth, gently and with affection. This action of the alpha says, "I am the leader." Dogs have lost this particular word of their mother tongue. In their domestic dialect, they lift a paw and place it on the shoulder of the lower-ranking individual to say they are the boss.

In response to the alpha wolf's statement of rank, the female licked his face and chin to tell him that he was indeed the leader, and a wonderful one at that. This pleased him. His tail flashed back and forth. I recalled my dog licking my hands and face and realized that those licks were not kisses but statements of my alpha rank.

The next communication came from the omega, a male in this case. He approached the alpha with his ears back and pressed tightly against his head, his mouth drawn down, his tail between his legs. The alpha lifted his head, wrinkled the top of his nose slightly, and pulled up his lip on one side to

"I'm boss."

"You're boss."

expose a single sharp, white canine tooth that contrasted with the black inner lip. The omega crouched lower, until his belly touched the ground, then rolled to his back. That is the pose of utmost canine humility; the omega was stating his rank, the bottom.

The beta trotted up, keeping his head and tail slightly lower than the alpha's, higher than the omega's, but at the same level as the alpha female's. The two of them seemed, in this situation, to be on a par. The alpha sniffed the beta's nose. Among wolves, the animal who sniffs first in the greeting ceremony is dominant. That word hasn't been lost. If, out walking your pet, you come upon a strange dog, you need not worry that it will be the aggressor if your dog sniffs it first. Like the wolf, he who sniffs first is boss.

As each wolf, in turn, exchanged greetings with the alpha, excitement grew. The pups jumped and ran among their elders. They nipped their tails and, if they could jump high enough, their ears and were patiently tolerated by the adults. One pup, carried away by the festive spirit, attacked the alpha. That would have called for severe discipline had it been an adult, but the old father simply looked at it condescendingly and wagged his tail.

GETTING DOWN TO WORK

The family greeting over, the alpha sat down, and the pack instantly gathered around him, their tails wagging furiously like pet dogs who gather around their master as he sits down to pull on his boots. The pups leaped, ran in circles, barked, bounced away and came back, acting exactly like my dog when I pick up the car keys. Something, the wolves were saying, was about to happen on the tundra along Sanctuary River.

The alpha threw back his head and howled a lugubrious note. It began low and crescendoed. The female joined in, then the beta and omega, each on his own note, each harmonizing with the others. This vocalization said pretty much what the prancing and jumping had said—"Something is going to happen"—but now to this was added, "Everyone get ready to cooperate." The howling reached a melodious climax, the pups joining in with high-pitched yipes, and, as I lay listening and watching, the treeless tundra in a bowl of mountains became a concert hall for the song of the wolves.

The howl given at this hour of the evening is called the *hunt song*, and it is sounded to coordinate the group and focus their attention on the job ahead. Dogs do not howl before a hunt, not even the foxhounds and beagles, for that song has been lost in breeding. Instead, they bark when the gun comes down from the rack or when the horses trot into the field for the same reason wolves howl their hunt song— to coordinate their activities and to psych themselves up for the hunt. Your pet may or may not bark when you pick up the car keys or put on your coat, but the other expressions are there—the wagging tail, bouncing, and running back and forth. When the ceremony was over on the tundra, the alpha led the adults over a ridge and out of sight, his fur flowing like a robe. The hunt was on.

HOME TALK

The pups, for all their exuberant participation, were left behind in the care of the omega. Wolves are devoted parents. The mother stays in the den with the newborns for the first two to five days in zoos and about ten days in the wild. During this time the father leaves food for her at the den entrance and pauses to listen to the sounds of life in the darkness, tilting his head and wagging his tail, passing on the message to the others that the pups are all right. They, getting the message, wag their tails too. Around the fifth day the mother may leave the pups to go off to feed on a kill, but she returns promptly to her charges. Her hunting skills, more than those of other pack members, are very closely integrated with the alpha male's, making her services so valuable that when the pups are between two and three weeks old and able to keep warm without her, the mother will join the hunters. Always before she goes, she assigns a baby-sitter; wolves never leave their pups unattended.

The female of Sanctuary River assigned the job to the omega, although the omega is not always the sitter and is only rarely a male, as in this case. When he attempted to follow the hunters, she came back over the ridge, met him, and, lifting her head and tail, loomed over him to display her rank. He refused to return. Both canine teeth gleamed from beneath her pulled-back lips. Her forehead creased in a frown. The omega cowered and slunk back to the pups.

For the next twelve hours they jumped on him, bit his tail and feet, knocked him over, and, when he lay down to rest, piled on him. Pester him as they did, they listened to him. When the baby-sitter spotted a hiker coming down the riverbank, he gave a bark of warning, and the pups disappeared into the tunnel.

Around 6:00 A.M., after an entire night of abuse, the omega walked to the ridge and stood stone-still. Then he wagged his tail slowly, and faster and faster until it was a blur. He apparently smelled or heard the hunters returning, for in less than a minute over the ridge and into camp they came. With that, the omega, relieved at last of his rambunctious charges, collapsed to the ground exhausted.

During their fourth week of age, the pups begin feeding

on partially digested food disgorged by the adults. The stimulus for the regurgitation can be the mere presence of pups or their begging actions—licking the corners of the adult's mouth, nuzzling its face, nipping at its jaws, or pawing the mouth and head. Age and parenthood have nothing to do with the response of a wolf to a pup's begging. A pair of year-old tame wolves disgorged food immediately upon seeing a litter of pups.

The babyish behavior of pups is the source of adult lick greeting, but you can notice with dogs that puppies are much more insistent on licking your face than they will be when mature. They try it on everyone, not just those few people to whom they will later be devoted.

WILD AND DOMESTIC SIMILARITIES

Children in a human family are tended by dogs much as wolves tend their young. They set themselves up as baby-sitters, and, if permitted, most will accompany youngsters to the school bus and out to play and will sleep on their beds to guard them like the mother wolf does. They also take all manner of abuse from these human pups, as does the wolf baby-sitter. I have seen little children pull the family dog's hair, bite it, pummel it, and roll on top of it without a word of protest from the dog, just a wry look of "This is how it is." Babies inspire special care from the family dog. My bluetick hound, Gunner, on hearing one of my infants cry would rush to me and stare until I did something about it. She guarded the baby buggy when an infant was in it, and although she never regurgitated food, she did heave the first day I introduced her to my screaming infant daughter.

Sometimes a wolf or dog will threaten unfairly and then apologize. In the Barrow lab I saw a pup run up to its mother and crawl between her legs to nurse. She turned and snapped but in the confusion of puppies disciplined the wrong one. She promptly apologized by smiling—pulling her lips back and opening her mouth slightly—and wagging her tail once. Dogs also apologize. When my Airedale snapped at me for trying to doctor a wound, she apologized for her aggressiveness by quickly relaxing her ears and opening her mouth. She wagged her stump tail—once. I accepted her apology by smiling, too, and shaking her muzzle in friendly dominance.

Two golden Labs that belong to my friend Kathy Kunhardt came into the living room where we were talking. Their ears were pressed back, their foreheads innocently smooth, and their tails wagged now and then, but very low.

"What are you apologizing for?" Kathy asked them and hurried to the kitchen. "They've taken a whole wheel of Brie off the table and eaten it!" she called in anger.

Kathy did not accept their apology but disciplined them with snarl words: "No, no, bad dogs. Bad." She stood above them to say this and shook her finger. She frowned and stared hard at them. They dropped into the submissive standing pose of the omega, pulled their tails in between their rear legs, lowered their heads, and drew their ears down, subdued—at least for the moment.

Discipline is the major subject in a wolf pup's schooling. It must learn what it can and cannot do, not only for its social welfare within the pack but for its safety on the trail, which is fraught with dangers: other wolves, human hunters, goring prey, bone-breaking crevasses, freezing weather, and long periods of starvation. Lessons begin early. If a pup wanders off, it is brought back by mouth. If it persists in straying as it grows older, it is growled at, then snapped at with teeth showing. Never does a mother wolf or dog bite a puppy. The threat of biting, conveyed by the bared-teeth threat face and the snapping gesture, subdues the pup as did Kathy's harshly spoken words and shaking finger. A pup is also disciplined by the mother standing above it, as she will do when siblings are fighting too strenuously. Her mere towering presence is sufficient to break up serious battles for dominance. A paw placed squarely on a pup's shoulder also subdues it. Once the rules are learned, the mother need only use her eyes, like the alpha male wolf, to get obedience.

Mother dogs use exactly the same vocabulary to discipline their young, and we use variations that share many of the aspects of canid talk. Kathy growled out her words, and she arose and stood above her dogs. Her lips were pulled down, and her teeth showed on the word "no." More important, she accepted the dogs' apologies sometime later, and the friendly bond characteristic of pack and human family was reestablished.

Both the discipline that you may have to give your dog and your acceptance of its apology will proceed with decorum if you remember that you are its alpha.

ON BEING AN ALPHA

And you *are* the alpha. When you take a pup from its parents or adopt an adult, the dog turns its love of the leader upon you. It needs no reward for this gift other than praise and affection. It has one happiness: to please you. You do not have to strike your dog for doing wrong. Your frowns, finger shakes, and sharp words are enough. You do not have to reward your dog with food. Your praise is its laurel. It wants to do what you wish it to do, to follow your commands, to hunt for you, guard your property, lie at your feet, be near you. The more you behave like an alpha, the more smoothly the relationship will go.

"How does a wolf alpha come to be?" I asked Dr. L. David Mech, the U.S. Fish and Wildlife Service wolf authority who is at Ely, Minnesota, studying some of the last of the great gray hunters in the lower forty-eight states.

"Very naturally," he answered. "They become alphas by becoming parents. Wolf pups, like children, look up to and obey their parents." That is the general rule, but in well-established packs many wolves do not breed, or if they are permitted to do so by the alpha, they are still subordinate to him, although boss to their own pups. Only when an alpha dies or becomes too decrepit to hold his position does a wolf get a chance to become the leader of the pack. To hold the position the alpha must constantly work at it. In an experiment an alpha removed from his semiwild pack for two weeks and returned at the end of that time never regained his leadership.

Some leaders reign for twelve, even fourteen, years, and during their tenure they may dominate the other males in their pack to prevent them from breeding. Just who these other members are was not known until Mech put radio collars on the wolves of Ely in the 1970s. Most are family, grown pups who have not left home, but some are young individuals who have taken off from their own families and have been invited to join another. Whether they are kin or foster members of the pack, they have to replace the boss if they are to become parents (and therefore alphas). The other alternative is for a male and female to go off and start their own family, in which case they are automatically alphas, but without the hunting support of others, that is difficult to do.

Dr. Michael Fox, an expert on wolf leadership, explained to me that puppies sort themselves into a hierarchy even before they struggle for status among the older members of the pack.

"There is an alpha in every litter of puppies," he said. "They emerge during the second, third, and fourth months, but sometimes as early as ten days, as the pups fight for dominance among themselves."

The alpha is always the largest, but when sizes look the same to you, the leader can be found by putting a bone in the midst of the pups. Dogs never fight over milk or any liquid and seldom attempt to defend a dish in which dry food is always present, but they will fight over a real bone from two weeks of age until the question of who is boss is decided at about eleven weeks. At that time the pup that has most often won, usually a male, becomes the alpha. After that time there may be no fight. The alpha will get to the bone first, and the others won't argue. The bone itself confers safety from the others' aggression. If you hold all the pups back but the omega and let it get the bone, the others will keep their distance even when you release them. It is understood, among dogs as among wolves, that food belongs to the one that claims it first, no matter what its status.

"All fighting stops when the alpha is established," Dr. Fox continued. "You can recognize him. He is fearless, initiates all the activities, and sticks to a job longer than the others." As a schoolteacher commented when I recounted these facts to her, "There's one in every classroom." She wasn't talking about bullies. A sign of the alpha is that he doesn't have to fight to get his way, and you, as an alpha, don't have to fight with your dog to get it to obey. The obligation of an alpha is to teach.

Dog training is not cruel and does not suppress individuality as some sentimentalists believe. It is an extension of the training a canid receives from its parents. Canid parents discipline their offspring with voice commands, gestures, facial expressions, eye contact, and combinations such as the threat stare, which is akin to the look your mother gave you when you were caught with your hand in the cookie jar. And they discipline for the same reasons we do—to make their offspring good citizens that are happily adjusted. There is little democracy among the social canids. They are alpha oriented, and happiness is doing what the leader wants them to do.

A well-trained dog is more alert, more communicative, and happier than one that is permitted to become a pest that must always be reprimanded for jumping on people, running away, eating off the table, knocking things over, and stealing objects from tables and counters. The dog that knows its alpha wants it to move back from the coffee table at cocktail time and lie down when told to do so is in tune with its heritage. You are the benevolent alpha, and all stress and argument ceases.

But people feel more conflict about pulling rank on a pup in order to teach it the rules of its family pack than an alpha wolf does. Edward Fouser, one of the first Seeing Eye dog trainers, who now specializes in training master and dog to communicate and work together, can train a three-month-old pup to heel, sit, and stay in one hour. It takes him eight hours of lessons when working with owners.

"I spend more time training the owner than I do the dog," he said. "Dogs learn quickly when they know what you want and are firm about it."

Whenever possible Fouser uses dogs' own language on them. He teaches a dog to stay within the confines of an area by placing a rope on the ground across driveways and escape routes. He leads the dog to the rope, pretends to trip over it, and yelps like a dog in pain. That yelp does it. The dog draws back and drops to its belly. Fouser picks up the rope, shakes it in front of the dog's face, and repeats, "No, no. Bad. Bad."

The dog does not move. Fouser steps across the rope and waits to see if the dog will follow. Most stay where they are, not crossing the forbidding and frightening barrier. If the dog does cross, Fouser snaps the collar and says, "No," again. That usually does it. Even my malamute, Qimmiq, who hates to stay, did drop to his belly and remain behind that rope, and to this day he remains behind other ropes he sees.

SURVIVAL SENSE

At least a dozen dogs in my hometown have been trained by Fouser to stay behind their boundary ropes even when they are covered with snow. There may be an additional motivation besides the yelp.

Wolves avoid murderous encounters with strangers from neighboring packs by leaving between territories a buffer zone where no wolf trespasses. L. David Mech, studying his radio-collared wolves at Ely, also discovered that the wolves do not hunt in these buffer zones. Because they don't, the buffer zones have come to serve as game preserves. They keep a few deer alive in times of stress when deer populations drop low. After killing off the animals on their territory, the wolves starve and die rather than hunt the buffer zones. The deer, protected from the wolves by their own social rules, begin to recover.

"The buffer zones," writes Mech, "tend to . . . form a reservoir for maintaining and recovering deer populations."

Keeping enemies at a distance with a no-man's-land keeps the predator-prey relationship balanced. And so Ed Fouser is able to teach dogs not to cross a rope—no-trespassing zones are not alien to their kind. You can also teach them to stay out of certain rooms by calling on their respect for boundaries.

The yelp is like the alarm cry of a bird that sends the flock to safety. I saw the mother wolf of Sanctuary River come romping with her pups to the top of a ridge within view of Gordon Haber and me. She looked down, saw us, and let out a wild high-pitched yelp as if in pain. The pups instantly turned and ran. A few moments later three pups returned to take another look at the curious two-legged animals. The next yelp from the female was bloodcurdling. After that we saw no more of the pups.

The yelp can be overused on dogs. They are canny, soon catch on that your "alarm" is insincere, and make their own judgments about a situation. But used for situations of genuine alarm it can be very effective.

THE ABCs

Dogs are clever at detecting insincerity, and if you are caught in duplicity, you are likely to endanger your status as an alpha. For instance, don't laugh at the mistakes your dog makes during training. It knows what a laugh is all about—fun—and with that all discipline breaks down. Qimmiq went spinning in circles when I laughed at his defiance of my request that he sit.

"Don't laugh!" Fouser admonished me. "The dog thinks you don't mean what you are saying—that lessons are funny. They're not." I snapped his collar, firmed my attitude, and Qimmiq sat.

Just as wolves send messages through eye contact, so do dogs, and so can you. When you are pleased, look into your dog's eyes. It will see your pleasure. But be sure of your mood. If you are angry with it, you will be giving an intimidating threat stare even if you are saying, "Nice doggie."

A kind gaze also helps a pup learn its name. Say the name while gazing into its eyes, brightly and with a smile. Repetition reinforces the identity you are transmitting to the pup through voice, eye contact, and your smiling, attentive face. The pup puts the whole thing together and arrives at a sense of self as early as two months. Now when its name is spoken, it looks at you. Eventually, if you are just talking about your dog in ordinary conversation to another person, it will prick its ears and listen. Dogs like to be talked about.

So easily does a dog learn its name that one wonders if wolves do not have names for each other, special barks to attract the attention of a specific individual. Certainly they have names for themselves. A wolf calling from a distance is immediately recognized by the members of its pack as well as by the members of neighboring packs. Who the wolf is determines how it is answered: ignored, howled to, or sought out.

The name you give your dog is important and should be picked carefully. Dogs like the sounds of hard "g" and "k," or at least they respond more quickly to these sounds than softer ones when tested. But the name should be to your liking and one to which you can give a variety of inflections, from soft to firm. "Butch," for example, is difficult to soften; "Willa" is hard to say firmly.

Dog trainers who have become famous for the apparent ease with which they get dogs to listen to them are like the great black alpha I watched that summer on the tundra. They are tolerant and affectionate, but more than anything they are exciting. Writes Barbara Woodhouse, the famous British dog trainer who dares to train dogs before the TV camera: "Giving praise and affection is where a multitude of owners fail their dogs. A pat and a kind word are not enough in the initial training of dogs; the atmosphere must be charged with a certain excitement, for dogs are very sensitive to excitement; when they have done right they love the wildest show of affection and a good romp. Dull owners make dull dogs."

Training is expedited by surprise. Trainers use the choke collar not to hurt but to snap pup or dog to attention. Keeping their attention is half the battle. Dogs tend to daydream, and the collar snap brings them back to reality. Said Fouser, "Training is communicating." You can't communicate with a daydreaming dog.

But you also have to know when not to invite a romp. Don't invite your dog to a game of chase when you are trying to teach it to come. To chase is to say to the dog, "Run away." Dogs chase when they see something fleeing, and they flee when something chases. Call "Come" and stand still. This takes enormous self-control when you see your dog ignoring

you and walking off, but it works. Be the alpha, call and
stand still; that is dog talk. Fouser can teach this command
in a few lessons.

Dogs learn our commands so readily when they are taught
correctly that they must have their counterparts in dogese.
The first time I told the pup Qimmiq to stay, he did so—and
I was mystified until I saw a golden Lab mother stop a pup
from pestering her. Her face, gestures, and attitude were not
unlike mine—mouth slightly open, eyes wide, feet firmly

a.

b.

c.

"Stay!"

planted, and body stock-still like a wolf that, detecting possible danger, freezes. I also held up my hand, a signal that dogs come to know even without a verbal command.

To teach your dog "Come," "Heel," "Stay," "Down," and "Off"—the basic commands every dog should know to be a good citizen—is not asking any more of it than the alpha asks the wolves of his crew. A look or a tail wag will summon a pup to its mother. The alpha glances over his shoulder at a juvenile that is gaining on him to hold it at "heel," and the "stay" signal can be a threat stare or a growl. To tell a lesser wolf "down," the alpha need only arise, lift his head and tail, and stand tall. Snarls suffice to keep a pup "off" the tail of a resting mother wolf. With these wolf words in mind I watched Fouser train a dog to heel. With a jerk on the choke collar, he got her attention. He gave the command and stepped forward. The dog pulled back. Fouser looked at the dog, jerked the collar, and looked into her now alert eyes. "Heel." His voice was quiet and low. He encouraged the little three-month-old when she came along. He was absolutely gentle, but firm. When she began to track along beside him, he used his wiggling fingers to keep her attention. Seeing the movement, she was diverted from a sudden preoccupation with another dog, looked up, got the friendly eye, and trotted on. Several months later I saw the dog heeling as her mistress walked along the road—no leash or choke collar on. There was a happy dog, I thought, following a strong leader because she had been told what to do and was pleased to find her role.

IN LOCO PARENTIS

Pups are not born knowing everything about how to be a dog, much less how to be man's best friend. They have much to learn from their parents. Although an old dog *can* learn new tricks, there are certain critical times when dogs learn certain things best, or most easily. Since we remove puppies from their mother (and they may never see their father at all) by as early as the sixth week, we are, like it or not, in loco parentis for a pup's first year.

Dog communications begin at birth when the mother, by licking her pup, stimulates it to breathe. First-time mothers may fail to give this crucial message; you may have to "tell" the pup to breathe by gently rubbing it with a terry-cloth towel.

The scent of the nipple is probably the second communication, a directional signal that guides the pup to nourishment. If unable to get the nipple, the puppy may utter its own first word—a high-pitched whimper, a call for help.

The signal for helplessness originates in clean-up time. The mother stimulates the pup to eliminate by licking its anal region, cleaning the puppy while nourishing herself. The pup usually rolls onto its back during this ritual, a pose that later

in life is a special mark of the omega but is also a dog's white-flag signal, which says that it has given up in a fight and, like a helpless baby, is not to be hurt.

The first few days of a puppy's life are spent feeding and sleeping. The mother does not leave the young for at least a few days, except to eat and eliminate—somewhat reminiscent of the mother wolf.

The eyes open between seven and ten days of age, and the pup wobbles forward on belly and feet. Probably by relying on its sense of smell, it can identify mother and keeper and can avoid strange objects. It yelps to say it is surprised, hurt, cold, or hungry. The mother usually responds to these cries, but people can begin talking to a pup by answering the needs. Pick it up and reassure it if something has surprised it. If it is cold or hungry, snuggle it back among its siblings and call the mother.

Dogs are not born loving us. This is taught by their mothers and handlers between the ages of four and fourteen weeks, the critical period when a dog becomes happily adjusted to people or remains forever shy and antisocial, like a wild thing. Pups raised without human contact flee with their tails low at the sight of people and are as elusive as wolves.

On the other hand, a pup that is taken from its mother and fed on a bottle before its eyes open becomes what breeders call "humanized." The pup ignores other dogs and behaves more like a person than a dog. When Stew, a bluetick hound, was six days old, he was put on a bottle by Emmy, the wife of George Norris, a fox hunter of Seneca, Maryland. I met Stew when he was about five years old. He did not bark at or run out to investigate other dogs, but sat on the porch and directed his attention to people's conversations, turning his gaze from face to face as the discourse flowed. He got to his feet when Emmy got to her feet, and he drank from the kitchen sink—no tin bowl for him. He slept in a bed and wagged his tail when Norris laughed, as if he shared the fun.

Willa, a mixed breed who belongs to my friend Melissa Young, is another bottle-raised dog who also thinks she is a person. When Melissa's friends come to visit, Willa walks serenely out of the house and greets them with a face smile— lips pulled back and up to expose all her teeth as people do when they smile. She was not taught this; she learned it her- self. She wrinkles her nose deeply, much as Melissa does when greeting her friends, and she escorts the guests to the living room. She sits down after they sit down.

At night Willa takes a "blanket," or comfort rag, to bed with her, preferably one of Melissa's old shirts or socks, which she sucks until she falls asleep. When Melissa's brother Andy visited her in North Carolina one spring, Willa took a shine to him and followed him everywhere, smiling, wrinkling her nose, and wagging her tail. Then Andy departed. She became depressed, her head drooped, her tail was down. Just before nightfall she passed the clothes hamper in the hallway, stopped, tipped it over, and, from the jumble of shirts, socks, and blue jeans, pulled out a T-shirt Andy had forgotten. She carried it to her bed, sucked on it, and was comforted.

"And she's very easy to talk to," said Melissa. "I simply explain what I am going to do with words and gestures—go to school for instance—and she trots to her bed and lies down.

"Occasionally she argues with me when I tell her she can't go to the store or that she's been bad—chewed up a shoe or something—but for the most part she understands and agrees."

Melissa did not pick this pup deliberately—Willa's mother had been killed by a car, and she took in the orphan. Breeders and behaviorists agree that the best family dogs are those raised by their mother with their siblings in a home where kids and adults pick them up and play with them. These pups develop affection for people and are interested in and relate to other dogs, being neither wild nor overhumanized.

During a puppy's early weeks its smelling apparatus is developing rapidly. It will approach a person slowly, nosing and sniffing shoes and clothing. A hand offered for smelling is an appropriate response, because scent "conversations" help to bond the puppy to you. The pup recognizes the individual odors of its siblings and parents as well as those of the humans who handle it, and it may cry if picked up by a stranger before it has had a chance to "sniff him out."

At this point the mother less often takes care of her puppies' elimination, and they will leave the nest to wander with their noses to the ground as they search for old odors of urine and feces. When they find such marks, the scent triggers the pups to eliminate. They don't care that the mark is on the rug or in the middle of the living room floor. The search can be a communication and can be used to housebreak a pup. As soon as it explores with its nose to the

ground, tell it where to eliminate by picking it up and putting it down on paper or outside. Paper with a trace of urine works wonders, the scent acting like quarters in a coffee vending machine.

One tainted paper can last a long time. I brought Qimmiq home a year after my Airedale, Jill, had been put away. The very first morning, he smelled an old mistake Jill had made on the rug as a pup twelve years before, squatted, and peed. There is only one remedy for that long-lived, urine-scented communication. Replace the rug.

About ten days after the pups leave the nest to eliminate, *following* behavior begins. The pup, without being given a command, instinctively follows its mother or another pup or a person for short distances—reminiscent of the wolves following behind the leader on the tundra. Speak to this development by leading the pup without a leash and repeating the word "heel." The earlier it hears this the better, even it if is not connecting the word with what it is doing. Your enthusiasm for its presence at your side can extend the behavior for longer and longer distances.

Although a pup learns from its mother from birth, beginning at about four weeks it has new capabilities for learning. By her own reactions the mother teaches the pup discrimination. It will turn its head at the sound of a familiar person and run from a stranger. It is now capable of making judgments and can discern the difference between danger and those things without significance. Evidence that enemies and dangers are taught by the mother comes from pups separated too early to learn such lessons. Willa, the bottle-raised pup, did not respond to a fire until she got a paw singed, whereas Qimmiq, who had lived with his mother for three months, drew back from fires but not from a hot electric plate, which his Arctic mother didn't know about. He was afraid of engines starting up but did not notice banging doors. Television was a harmless curiosity, which he gazed at without concern even when it crackled with the sound of gunfire. His mother had been trained not to shy at such sounds. This period of intense learning, which lasts about a month, is a good time to intensify communication with a pup. The month-old pup can bark to demand attention or announce a stranger. Answer its request for attention by stroking it with the same soothing movements of its mother's tongue. Praise it for announcing a stranger with a pat and some enthusiastic words. It can use its sense of smell to track down food and family—your clue that it is time to call the pup to dinner or to play. The pup's feelings become easier to read. It can wag its tail to acknowledge living things. It can wrinkle its forehead, one of the first of the complex facial expressions that will develop.

THE MAKING OF A BEST FRIEND

Between the fourth and thirteenth weeks is the best time to establish a relationship with the pup, or, as behaviorists say, *socialize* it. Pick up and fondle the pup every day, talking to it to make it comfortable with humans. Early handling will save months of work later on, and some pups cannot be socialized at all if the process is begun after four months, when it may be too late to interact with people.

Aggression can be handled right out of a pup's personality in this same period if a mild-mannered dog is what you want. This is the time when siblings are fighting for dominance. Behaviorist John Paul Scott and his students at the University of Chicago stopped pups from fighting by picking them up every time they tangled. Diverted by being off the ground, they instantly quieted down. After the tenth week they did not fight at all. By six months they were unusually nonaggressive pups. "Don't fight," you are saying by picking up a scrapping pup during this period.

On the other hand, letting them fight will give you a clearer idea of which is going to be the alpha, which the omega. The alpha will eventually fare best in the family that appreciates its alertness, courage, initiative, and stick-to-itiveness. Both male and female alphas learn quicker and are more intelligent. An omega makes a better dog for working people who do not have much time to interact with it. Omegas, which are often the smallest in their litter, are pleasant dogs, relatively nonaggressive, and often shy. Omegas make lovable pets.

Many people consider six weeks a pretty good time to find homes for puppies—perhaps because the mother is neither nursing them nor cleaning up after them at that point, and the alpha human keeper is degraded to the role of a babysitter. But five to six weeks is a particularly vulnerable time for the puppies. They are learning to fear those things their mother fears, as well as developing a few fears of their own. They will draw back or run away when a person walks rapidly and noisily toward them, even though they had not reacted in fear to that person a week before. Each pup is also becoming an individual, and its new ability to make independent judgments is equaled by its new susceptibility to psychological damage based on its unique experiences. If it is hurt or badly scared by people during these weeks, it may never overcome its fear of people. With this vulnerability comes a strong attachment to place, so if it is taken from its home, it is all the more unsure of itself. Your word to the pup now is gentle hands and slow, not fast, movements.

If you are going to keep a puppy yourself, use the strengthening of its interest in following through weeks five to nine to introduce the leash. The pup will track along nicely

PUPPIES' SOCIAL PROGRESS CHART

During the first 4 weeks the puppy is more interested in its mother than in people.

Week 1   Sleeps, nurses, yelps when hungry, hurt, or cold

Week 2   Eyes and ears open, lifts belly from ground to walk

Week 3   Leaves nest to urinate

Yelps when restrained or when removed from mother and litter mates

Gives earsplitting yelps when removed to a strange place

Fights playfully with litter mates

Week 4   Follows mother, litter mates, or person

Approaches a person slowly and wags tail

Startles at sudden sounds and movements

Weeks 5 thru 13 are the period of socialization when puppies that are handled daily adjust well to people. The most critical period is week 5 and week 6. Ups and downs characterize this time, so leash training is best done during alternate weeks 5, 7, and 9. House training can begin during week 8.

Week 5   Weaning begins

---

without being yanked, but do encourage it to walk on your left, and use the word "heel" with spirit and enjoyment.

Pack movement begins around two months. This is not just following. Suddenly, without being led, all the pups rush to the door or gate in one tumbling mass. Since we discourage pack movement in our dogs, there is no reason to talk to this development. Observe and enjoy it; a mass of puppies coming toward you is wonderful.

Two months, or even a bit earlier, is the natural time to teach the word "no." During weaning between five and

	Learns first fears from mother
	May become fearful of handler
Week 6	Becomes curious about new people and dogs
	Becomes emotionally sensitive and may be susceptible to psychological damage
Week 7	Weaning is completed
	Begins to attack other pups by ganging up
Week 8	Uses definite spot to defecate far from food, will not defecate if shut up overnight, and sniffs for a spot to urinate where there is a trace of urine scent
Week 9	Chases and catches other pups and toys
	Fear of handler disappears with daily handling
Week 10	Hierarchy within litter established, serious fighting ceases
Week 11	Hunting behavior begins
	Anxiety in strange places eases
Week 12	Makes the best transition to a new home

For better or worse, 13 weeks marks the end of the period during which a pup can be optimally socialized. By 14 weeks, when the pup is accustomed to its new home, training to "Heel," "Sit," "Down," "Stay," and "Come" can begin.

seven weeks, the pup has learned the meaning of "no" from its mother. Hers is the growl-bark plus the wrinkled nose and the drawn-up lips that expose her canine teeth. She snaps close to a pup's face but never bites. You can come pretty close to the dog "no" by lifting your own lips in a menacing grimace and jutting your face toward the puppy as you growl-bark, "NO."

At twelve weeks hunting behavior is emerging, and with it a readiness for new experiences. That's the age when the wolf parents move their offspring from the nursery den to

summer camp, when the puppies begin to exuberantly practice hunting games on the patient baby-sitter, and when they
begin to participate in the greeting ceremony that will bind
them to their alpha and the pack.

Breeders agree that sixteen weeks of age is the ideal time
for puppies to leave for their new homes, not only because
the puppy is more sure of itself by then, but because pro-
spective owners can tell more about its personality.

Dog pups, like wolves at the same age, lose at this point
their strong attachment for the first home place—enthusiastically practice hunting skills with balls and sticks—and
look to whoever seems to be in charge for love and leadership.
This is not necessarily the person who feeds the pup, as many
people think, but the one who most clearly teaches the puppy
how to behave, and that can be a child.

Not that leaving home and pack is easy. When I took
Qimmiq from his mother, he buried his head in my arms and
kept it there as I walked home through Barrow's snowy streets.
He would not look at me. He was eight weeks old, a month
younger than the ideal time for separation, and stoic. He made
no sound when I put him down on the floor of the house.
After a long look around him he searched for his mother,
nose held high as he ran sniffing for her scent. I petted him
and called his name, but he acted as if I were not there. His
eyes had the look of the daydreamer, seeing without seeing.

The next day he gave up the search for his mother but
still buried his head in my armpit when I picked him up. I
talked to him, whimpered to him, sang to him, and after a
few minutes he slowly lifted his head and focused one yel-
lowish brown eye on my furless face and then on my blue
eyes. He seemed to be registering me on his consciousness at
last—and I was in his world. He cuddled against my body.

Thereafter he was a domestic dog.

THE EYES HAVE IT

I have become convinced that eye contact with dogs, as with people and wolves, is loaded with meaning. Qimmiq would not give me his gaze until he was ready to shift his love to a new leader figure, but once he took me in through his eyes and bestowed upon me those deep instinctive feelings that are love, his flashing glances kept us in contact from then on.

When I take Qimmiq to the woods to let him run and bound over logs and rocks like a deer, he comes back, gets my eye, sees me nod, "I'm okay, go on" while looking him in the eye, and then turns and dashes off again. When strangers enter the house, he looks at me, I signal with my eyes, "This is a friend," and he comes forward wagging his tail. Whenever I go in and out of the front porch where he spends much of his time, I take his chin in my hand and look lovingly into his eyes. He looks back, his ears go down in deference, and his tongue comes out as if to lick. He loves to wander like his near kin the wolves, but I can get him to come back to me if, when I call his name, he turns toward me. I catch his eye and lock his gaze with my threat stare. With reluctance, for he is still a pup, he slinks toward me. If he really does not want to come, he will avoid my eyes and bounce on as if he did not hear.

I tell him many things with my eyes: that I am busy and cannot play, that he cannot come with me in the car, that he is beautiful, that I like to have him with me. You don't need words, although I often use them, for, to a dog, your eyes brim with meaning.

THE LANGUAGE OF SCENTS

Many puppies announce their adolescence at about six months by taking a first long excursion from home. This urge can be indulged where there are no leash laws, for the explorer will come home. However, Coco, a brown poodle in my hometown, off on her first juvenile excursion, was picked up by the dogcatcher, and her mistress was fined twenty-five dollars.

Adolescence lasts for two or three months, culminating for the female in the first estrous period at around eight months. Estrus, the period that ends in several days of fertility, is marked by the emission of blood and a change in behavior. The female is more affectionate, whimpers restlessly, and urinates more frequently than usual.

The male adolescent pup begins lifting his leg to urinate in the manner of the adult canid. Although he may long ago have settled dominance matters with his peers, his elders no longer consider him a "mere puppy," and he may have to scrap with other dogs in the neighborhood until his position is established in this wider world.

Both the sexual status of females and the social status of males are advertised by scent. A dog's smell receptor cells bear a number of fine hairs at their surface that pick up chemicals and report them to the brain. A dog has more than a million of these hairs, giving it the capacity to discriminate among thousands of smells in doses many hundreds of times more diluted than a human could detect. On a scale of one to ten, our ability to pick up odors is two compared with the dog's ten.

Scientists believe that scents tell dogs more about the world than any of their other sensory organs. We have such poor noses that we are ignorant of almost all of the information dogs read as easily as we read a newspaper. Chemicals that lie in footprints tell the species, sex, and emotional state of the printer; the odor of a storm blowing on the wind sends the reader to shelter. Unfortunately, that avenue of communication is a one-way street to us, for although we apparently communicate information about ourselves to dogs, scent is the medium we understand the least. We stumble along on eyesight, while our hound presses its nose to the ground and runs off through the woods on the scent of a deer as if it were following Interstate 80.

I learned about the odors of the field and forest from Gunner, my bluetick hound. They are exciting, she said with her hysterical barks. They are also hot, cold, in the air, on the ground, old and faint, new and vivid. As I watched her run and listened to her report, I thought that to her those invisible scents must have been presences with shapes and textures. She said so with her voice. A hot trail was a high yipe, yipe; a cold trail was a bark given now and then. Once, she announced with a series of yipes a scent so fresh and inviting that I dropped to all fours and sniffed the earth. There was no odor of the furry footstep of a rabbit for me, let alone the aroma of its being startled from sleep or the smell of its fear as it fled—only the scent of dry earth.

Realizing that scent is a foreign language to us, we have bred dogs to be our translators when we are in the field and forest. Their voices ring out announcing the presence of game and direct the human hunter to it. This communication between hound and human did not come from the wolves— they hunt silently. Wolves approach their prey without a sound to surprise it. As they move, each one keeps its eye on the leader and, in silence, makes up its mind what part it shall play in the stalk and kill. Even the kill is quiet. A good voice on the trail was selectively bred for in the dog. A call from the briars and dense thickets, "I'm on the trail of a rabbit," was much more valuable to us than wolves' noiseless strategies.

Dogs do translate by bark the kind of prey they smell, and some also listen for our spoken commands to know what prey we seek. Having a dog is the next best thing to having a good nose. My father used to discuss what was afoot in the Potomac River bottomlands with his hound dog, Spike. He would tell him, "Hunt up a squirrel," and Spike would circle the forest until he picked up a squirrel scent. He would run the animal up a tree and announce it until Dad caught up. Spike found a raccoon when my father wanted a raccoon and deer when he wanted a deer. When they were simply out to investigate the forest and learn what was around, Spike would tell Dad what scent he had come upon. He had a different voice for each animal. A rabbit was a high yipe, a raccoon a series of sharp barks, a squirrel a low yip, and a deer—well, that was a rapidly fired succession of barks, yipes, and bellows, a dog's name for the quintessential odor.

PUBLISHING THE NEWS

That is the receiving side of scent. On the transmission side is *scent marking*—the leg lifting of males, the urine ads of females in heat, the depositing of feces, and the spreading of gland secretions that broadcast to other dogs just who the marker is and what it is up to.

Scent marking is the paramount language of the canids. Over the eons it has become ritualized, the male lifting his leg to shoot his message high and far, the female, or bitch, squatting. One of the canids, the bush dog, carries the ceremony to the extreme. The male walks his hind feet up a tree as high as he can while balancing on his front feet, then squirts.

The ritual of the domestic dog includes methodically marking vertical objects, such as trees and fire hydrants; odors on the ground, such as that of a carcass or the urine of a female; and new things in the environment, such as a paper cup that has been recently dropped, a newspaper pitched up on the porch, or a new chair set out in the yard.

The male uses three positions: standing with one hind leg raised and crooked when squirting on a vertical object, standing with all legs spread apart to mark the ground, and the same pose with one leg slightly lifted. Females, who scent mark less frequently, sometimes lift a hind leg under the body as they squat.

Since we can't really know what dogs are saying in these messages, animal behaviorists have come to conclusions by observing what they mark and how other dogs react to the message. Said Swiss ethologist Rudolf Schenkel, one of the first to study scent marking, "Canid scent marking is a social

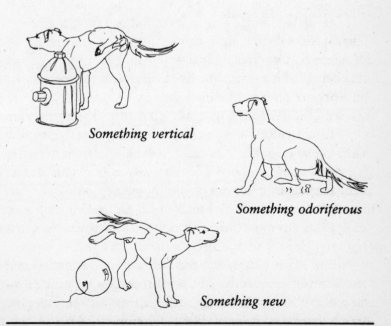

Something vertical

Something odoriferous

Something new

act that defines the territory, makes acquaintances, forms pairs and legitimizes the alpha's position."

British scientist M. Lyall-Watson concludes that an animal's scent on posts and objects maintains its familiarity with the countryside. A dog that roams a street each day seeks out and finds its own scent on a garbage can or automobile tire and is reassured by the familiarity of the posts it has "colored." It jogs along loosely, confident. If, however, it steps into new country, it becomes nervous and marks liberally to make the unknown familiar. Its making odoriferous marks is like our blazing the trees in a strange forest to find our way in and out. The scent reassures the dog as the blaze reassures the man, and the landscape becomes as nice as the sight of your street after a long trip.

Scientists think that the canid family can tell from urine scent alone who the urinator is, its sex, age, health, what it has been eating, and whether its mood is angry, fearful, or content. After sniffing up a news report from a neighboring dog, a male—less often a bitch—tops that with his mark and information of his own. The fire hydrants and lampposts of the block are gossip columns for dogs.

And, like wolves, dogs mark a territory. The borders are learned from you. When you step off your property, the dog senses a change in your attitude. It will bark to warn strangers from your home turf but will not bark as ferociously, if at all, on the sidewalk in front of your house or apartment. That is common ground. When I walked Jill off the property onto the road, her smooth forehead tightened, her neck lowered ever so slightly, and she became less frisky as she lost her confidence off her land. She did not bark at other dogs and scent marked frequently. On her property she urinated to empty her bladder but rarely let fall the few drops at a time that are typical of scent marking. When I put her in the car, however, her self-assurance returned. I had conveyed somehow through my attitude that this was home turf, too. She barked as murderously at dogs and people from "her" car as she did from "her" house.

Evolutionists speculate that scent marking grew from a fear reaction. Young puppies removed from their nest to a strange place urinate out of fear. It seems likely that that is a remnant of the behavior primitive canids practiced even as adults. Eventually the urine mark became useful. Other canids coming upon it either kept their distance or, looking for a mate or companion, approached. As for the marker, when it circled back and found the smell of itself, it was reassured. The foreign territory was familiar. It had been there before.

As scent marking evolved, the male canid ritualized the behavior by lifting his leg, probably to hit high and show how big he was, and by saving squirts to top another's squirt, a crude measure of status. Today, an individual's blatant newscasts on a city fire hydrant can read, "I am big. I am male. I am young. I am confident. I am irritable. I am off my property."

TALKING SCENTS

Given the power of scent communication, there is scarcely a naturalist who has not tried to speak to wild canids through this medium in and around the campsite. Farley Mowat, author and naturalist, is one of the more successful experimenters. Observing that wolves scent marked the perimeters of their property to keep off other wolves, Mowat marked off an area around his Canadian campsite in the manner of the wolf. As he reports in his wonderful book *Never Cry Wolf*, the wolves got the message and respected his space. L. David Mech, on the other hand, who was also inspired to scent mark his campsite while studying the wolves of Isle Royale, Michigan, got nowhere. "They paid little if any attention to my mark," he said.

Dogs also ignore human urine. No one knows why. Maybe humans say nothing in their urine, or maybe dogs know we can't smell their answers anyway, so why bother?

The number of times a male scent marks, most dog owners agree, is an indication of just how macho the pee-er is. A terrier named Butch was taken to Japan by my neighbors Sis and Jay Melvin. When Sis walked him in the streets of Tokyo, he marked objects constantly, "Every foot or so," she said. "It took forever to walk a block. One day I kept tabs. I counted 109 pees, and he was still going when I finally dragged him home. What a male." But I suspect his many pees also indicated his nervousness on those foreign streets, for dogs scent mark frequently when under stress.

Feces marking by dogs is both odoriferous and visual and, consequently, a louder statement than the liquid one. This mark is not used as frequently as urination, feces usually being hidden. When it is used, however, you cannot miss it, for it is put down to attract attention. Dogs competing for our female left their visual marks on stones, in the middle of the drive, and even perched on flower pots.

Scientists consider feces display to be a part of scent marking that also arose from automatic responses and evolved into a way of familiarizing the animal with the environment. That, they agree, is the first function. Secondarily, feces marking, like urination, is a social display that brings the sexes together, maintains the territory, and, therefore, is an important function in the survival of the species. That, I agree, is why my yard was so odorously decorated.

Anyone who has walked a dog on a leash and tried to curb it when other dog feces adorn the sidewalk has seen the visual importance of feces. The dog sees, sniffs, identifies the depositor, and carefully selects a spot nearby to put its mark. Both males and females scratch the ground with forelegs and hind legs after feces marking, but it is more common in males. With firm strokes of their feet they leave these inscriptions for their neighbors to see. On loam and in grassy yards the scratches and feces become a signature. I can identify the marks of two dogs in my neighborhood by their scratches and piles. Barney, a long-legged hound, has a deep, long scratch that invariably makes a V and digs up the turf. His feces are large and piled up. Jerry's piles are smaller and more strewn. His scratches are short, numerous, and shallow.

Some dog observers are pretty sure feces are placed by dogs as a pointed remark to their owner. Nele left her pile mark on a bed when her mistress scolded her harshly one day. Corky, a farm dog in Michigan, left his feces on the back-porch step for his master to see when pups (not his) born to the coonhound bitch got more attention than he did.

Rubbing parts of the body—head, neck, rump, side— on the ground and on other individuals is another kind of scent marking. All canids emit a personal scent, which can be released by fear but is more often offered up in affection. My Airedale would perfume the air with her "doggie smell," as people call it, when I came home after a long trip. She also emitted her scent when I was being particularly affectionate— holding her head in my hands, hugging her, kissing her nose. It was her way of saying what I was saying—"I love you."

Wolves and some dogs like the malamute have a gland on the top surface of the tail about four inches from the root. By rubbing their chin and cheeks on this gland and then rubbing their face against other members of the pack, which also contribute their gland perfumes, they mix individual scents to concoct a family odor. A wandering wolf knows when it is home by the ambrosia of its pack on the wind.

Rolling in (to us) foul-smelling scent is another olfactory joy of the canids. I always considered it a bad habit of an ill-trained dog until I was set straight by Michael Fox.

"Scent rolling is an esthetic thing," he said. "Dogs and wolves will roll in raunchy odors just so they can wear a different and exciting smell. It brings attention to themselves. All the other wolves and dogs come up to smell and investigate.

"Like your wearing a new dress," he added.

After Qimmiq came home one day smelling of dead fish, I asked trainer Ed Fouser if there was a way to stop a dog from rolling in scent. He shook his head—"Keep him on a leash."

BODY LANGUAGE

When a person travels in a foreign land where he doesn't understand a word of the language, he can nevertheless communicate. He can see in a face whether he is to laugh at a joke or commiserate with sadness, approach in friendliness or be on guard against antagonism. And, knowing in general how human societies work, he isn't altogether baffled by what's going on around him. We may not be able to read canine gossip columns as they are posted on neighborhood fire hydrants, but by understanding social context and body language, we can guess our dog's feelings and be a better friend.

Your dog's social position is easy to see in its facial expression, posture, and movements. A dominant dog says it is boss by holding its head high like a monarch, its tail up and erect. It thrusts its chest forward and walks stiff legged, in almost a military stride. It may *ride up*—put a paw on the shoulder of a lesser-ranking individual to get its head above the other's and declare itself boss.

Dogs that are not as high ranking hold their heads and tails lower when they meet their superiors. Like the omega wolf, the lowest-ranking dog greets a more dominant dog with its head down and its tail between its legs. Its jaw sags and its eyes partially close. It is the embodiment of the phrase "hangdog look." When challenged, the omega dog rolls over on its back and surrenders.

The regal posture of dominant dogs, male or female, is accompanied by lordly facial expressions. Bosses wear smooth foreheads and wide-open eyes. Both the large eyes and the smooth expanse make the head appear larger. Their muzzles, too, are smooth, and their lips are relaxed.

Facial expressions change to signal a dog's mood and intentions, regardless of its social status. Therefore you can't rely on body posture alone; facial expression can modify the body's meaning. For example, the pose of the coward or dog who has been abused, is, at the sight of the enemy, back arched, rump pulled down and tucked under. But this is also the pose taken by a pup when asking an elder to play and a prelude to greeting man or dog friend when awakening from sleep. The face makes the difference. The coward holds its ears back and down, mouth closed, and eyes narrowed. The play-seeking pup is wide-eyed and smooth-faced. The awakening dog yawns as it arches.

The meaning of another gesture can only be guessed by context. The lion crouch, down on the belly with head held low to the ground like a lion stalking is intended to terrify an opponent when confronting it. The bitch also uses this pose when approaching her mate, and English shepherds will fall into the lion crouch when chasing balls or rounding up sheep. It expresses readiness for just about anything, and only the context can tell you what.

THE DOG'S MAJOR FACIAL EXPRESSIONS

Relaxed and confident

Ears
back

Worried

Wrinkled brow

Suspicious

*Lowered
ears*

Threat stare

Lips pulled back

Somewhat fearful

Fangs
bared

*Extremely fearful and
threatening to bite*

Apologetic

HEADFIRST

But there are facial expressions that carry specific meanings.

The full threat expression, "Get back!" is said with bared teeth, opened mouth with corners pulled forward, and a wrinkled head with ears erect and pointed forward.

Closed mouth with corners pulled far back, a smooth forehead with slitlike eyes, and ears drawn far back and close to the head is the face of the insecure—"I am afraid."

Suspicion is communicated by holding the ears out to the side and slightly down; the eyes are half-closed, the forehead creased between the eyes. The lips are raised only enough to slightly wrinkle the nose. The mouth is closed, and the corners are pulled downward.

The dog's emotional expressions of anxiety, happiness, peace of mind, anger, affection, jealousy, embarrassment, and hostility are not too different from our own ways of communicating our feelings by face and body. The ability of the dog to read our feelings seems like mental telepathy until we observe what we are saying with body and face.

My young friend Paul has a dog who lies down beside him when he is sick in bed with a cold or fever, but not when he is in bed relaxing or reading.

"When I'm sick, I look sick," Paul said after thinking about why his dog behaved as he did. "I droop and drag around, and Skip knows—just like I know when he's sick."

When the setter down the street got into the garbage, as he did from time to time, he would look at his mistress and sulk before she could open her mouth to reprimand him.

"My anger is written all over me," she said. "I finally realized my face talks to my dog. I scowl, I jut out my chin ever so slightly, clamp my lips together, and draw myself up when I'm mad at him.

"I don't need words. I've said them."

An embarrassed or guilty dog won't look you in the eye any more than will a child who knows he has done wrong. A wildly happy dog can't clamp its mouth glumly shut any more than you can when you're bursting with joy. What's more, glum and happy moods are catching. Laugh and your dog laughs with you, even though it doesn't get the joke.

SUBTLETIES AND EMPHASES

The dog, in its adjustment to man, has evolved a few expressions especially for us. Lip licking means the dog is under stress and that possibly you and it are not communicating. You may be giving orders the dog does not understand.

Jaw tremors express intense emotion. My Airedale quivered her lower jaw when I brought another dog into the house, when she smelled a deer on the wind, when she heard a record of wolves howling, and when she looked upon a human infant.

Panting is another expression that has evolved, finally, to contact us. Originally it was only a device to expel heat from the body; then it was that plus a means of communicating to its own kind anticipated exertion. A pup that wants its parent to play runs in a circle with its rear end tucked under and its back arched. If the parent does not respond, the pup will stop, face the adult, and pant. It is not perspiring because it is overheated but because it is saying, "Play with me." Play generates heat, heat generates panting. What was originally an end, panting from exertion, has become a symbol for activity. It is used on us with more specific meanings. Spike, my father's hunting dog, panted when he saw him take down the gun from the rack in the living room. He was talking about the miles he would be covering on the trail of a fox or a deer. He was saying, as my father interpreted it, "Let's go hunting." Nele literally pants for cookies, even though that form of hunting requires hardly any exertion.

Such indirect communications between man and dog are most evident when it comes to going out in the car, and just about every dog owner speculates about what it is that sends his pet bolting to the door before he even picks up the keys. Like myself, many set up elaborate experiments to find out.

For years I thought it was the jingling of the car keys that sent the Airedale to the door. Once, I purposely left the keys in the car so that she would not hear them. The next day, I had no sooner decided to go to the store than she was at the door. I decided the signal was the putting on of my coat. The next day, I wore a sweater so that I would not have to put on a coat. When I was ready to go to the store, Jill got up and went to the door without a word or a whistle from me. I decided it must be the combing of my hair. I did not comb my hair the next day before going out. She was at the door. I thought it was the time of day. I did not take the car out for two days, although I opened the door and went into the garden. She did not rush to the door in excitement but followed me to the garden with loyal boredom.

Finally I began observing my movements and my facial expressions and realized I was telling her my plans with very subtle signals. I shuffle my feet a little bit when I have decided to go downtown in the car. I also leave what I am doing with a resolute movement as compared with the casual way I get up from the word processor or stop what I am doing when I am not going anywhere. But more important, I am definitely wearing my "I'm-going-to-get-in-the-car" pose and face—a straightening of the back and an absentminded open mouth as I think about what I have to do in town.

Of course, Jill took cues from my clothing, just as all dogs do. Putting on my mountain boots would send her to the door, sometimes hours before I was ready to go hiking. When I dressed in suit, high heels, and business coat, my straightened back and absentminded expression didn't fool her. My clothes said, "No dog." Sometimes she never bothered to lift her head from the rug when I went out the door in my city clothes.

We don't have the advantage of reading from a dog's

clothing what it has on its mind for that day, but shades of meaning are emphasized by a dog's face and body coloration. The dark nose, the light belly, dark trim on the ears and necks are somewhat akin to punctuation. The colors emphasize what is being said on the face and with the body. We use body punctuation also—lipstick, mustaches, jewelry, and hats. With them we emphasize our personalities or punctuate the message we want to get across. "I am sexually attractive" is one of the more obvious.

Dogs (with the exception of those bred for a solid coloration) have darker hair on the muzzle, forehead, around the eyes, along the rims and at the base of the ears, and on the tail. The inner lip is usually black. Pale hairs grow inside the ears and on the belly.

It was once thought that a pale underside simply meant a lack of pigmentation-stimulating sunshine on the underside of the animal, but no matter how it came to be, it is now in the language. The omega that flops in submission exposes its white fur—the white flag of surrender—to say, "I give up. Don't hurt me." Aggression is turned off as though by a switch; the aggressor stops its attack. No wolf can attack an individual that is flashing this signal of surrender, but, unhappily, the signal has descended in somewhat garbled form to dogs, and there are those that do not honor it.

Most do, even if the signaler is a one-color dog that lacks contrast between the belly and the rest of the body. The belly-up pose is sufficient. When Jill visited Sadie, an apricot-all-over poodle, Sadie rolled onto her back at the sight of one toothy display from Jill. Jill's face relaxed; she lost her desire to fight, turned, and trotted off.

Facial coloration emphasizes what is being said there. The dark hairs on the forehead gather together when the animal frowns, becoming darker as they are compressed into furrows. The displeasure is more clearly visible with this emphasis. The black inner lip contrasts sharply with the white canine teeth, so that when the lip is lifted, the cruel fangs draw the eye and inspire fear. The meaning stands out as if in quotes.

Black hairs on the dog's tail draw attention to that bold signaler, and raised hackles on the back are more prominent for their dark coloration, which contrasts with the lighter underfur. The inner ear has light-colored fur margined with darker fur—black or dark brown. The outlines make the expressive positions of the ears more easily seen.

STREET TALK—BOSS TO BOSS

The best way to learn what your dog is saying with face and body is to take a walk with it in a neighborhood where dogs abound and see how it speaks to its own kind.

Dog conversations always begin with the greeting, which varies slightly depending on the status, sex, and the social relationship of the dogs. I took notes one day on the greeting between two boss males who knew each other.

The two came trotting up to one another. Both were confident, their heads and tails were held high, their foreheads were smooth as each brandished his alpha title. As they came together, they stiffened their front legs and lifted their heads and tails to get them higher than the other's. They were pretty equal.

Their eyes were round, their ears erect and partly forward. Suddenly they rushed together and stood head to tail, freely offering their rumps for an anal sniff. This was an act of confidence on both their parts. Insecure dogs keep their rear ends from being sniffed by lowering their tails and circling.

Two boss dogs greeting

The tension was building. I wondered who would give in first. The faces began to wrinkle. Creases appeared in the smooth foreheads. Confidence was eroding in both animals, but they were still equal. Simultaneously they lifted their lips to expose their wicked fangs, which gleamed against their black lips. They were both wearing the threat face, ready to attack. They wrinkled their noses, expressing anxiety. As they did so, they raised their hackles, making themselves appear larger, and growled. In dog talk the deeper the growl, the more dominant the individual, and each was trying to hit the basement of sound. This fact is useful when being firm with your dog. A deepened voice conveys your dominance in the situation.

The two boss dogs looked as if they were going to kill, and I stepped back a few feet.

The dogs circled, still flank to flank. Their foreheads were wrinkled both horizontally and vertically, the dark hairs on their faces making the lines more visible as they gathered in the grooves.

Posing alike, the bosses maintained the balance of power but were looking for a way out, "with honor," as they rolled their eyes to search for excuses to depart—a bird, a master, another dog.

Some subtle signals were exchanged that I couldn't detect, because, although they were still circling, they were stepping apart equally, as if by mutual agreement.

When they were ten feet apart, each, keeping an eye on the other, walked off, slowly at first, then faster and faster. They lifted their legs and peed simultaneously. Neither had to say, "I lose." Their faces relaxed as they walked off stiff legged, each saying he was boss dog.

PAL TO PAL

When two male friends meet, one of whom has already established his dominance, the greeting is much more relaxed. Major, a dominant dog, and Barney rushed to meet each other, tails wagging. Major sniffed nose, groin, and tail first. Then he permitted Barney to sniff his nose, groin, and tail while holding his head and tail higher than his friend's. There was no show of teeth, no contest. After gathering all the news about each other, they went off a short distance and urinated. That done, they put their signatures on the ground—deep claw marks made with front and back paws. Major and Barney then trotted off together down the lane.

Males do not fight females, and most will take outrageous abuse from a bitch with tolerance and forbearance. When Lucky, my dog Gunner's favorite mate (dogs are faithful if given a choice of mates), came to visit in the off-season, she would snap at Gunner, growl, and knock his feet out from under him. He replied by courteously wagging his tail and coming back for more.

BITCH TO BITCH

Two females, however, will tear into each other, particularly if they are terriers.

Jill, the Airedale terrier, and Koda, who was part terrier and who lived on the other side of my woods, were both fighters—and enemies. One encounter went like this:

Jill saw Koda approaching and ran to meet her as she came over the border into our yard. She permitted her to come about twenty feet onto our property, thus getting the advantage of having her enemy on her own turf. (Among birds and some mammals the individual fighting on its own property always wins.)

Koda dropped into the lion crouch and stared at Jill. Jill answered by keeping her face smooth, announcing the alpha she was (on her own turf), and asserted her dominance by pulling her ears forward. Koda crept forward on her belly for the kill. Jill flaunted her rear end to show just how confident and dominant she was. Koda responded by leaping to her feet. They rushed together and stood side by side, heads to tails. They growled, trying to bluff each other out. Minutes passed as they waited to see who would chicken out first. Jill took the offensive by showing not just one canine tooth but both. Her nose wrinkled. "Your life is not worth a bone chip," she was saying.

The talk moved to the ears and the corners of the mouth. Jill's ears stood up as far as she could get them, her mouth opened, and her lips lifted clear of all her front teeth as she put on the intense threat face. "I'm not afraid of you. Beware of me!"

Koda was intimidated by this show of power. She drew her ears slightly back. Her mouth pulled downward like a frightened child's. She snarled. Jill's ears went back for an instant in a quick admission of a lack of confidence in herself, then she gained control and shot them forward. She growled. Her growl was deeper than Koda's.

I walked toward the dogs hoping to prevent a fight. Jill

gave me the eye, asking me to do something before another bloody battle broke out between the two of them.

I had two choices: lunge at Koda, which might have triggered Jill to attack, or stand between them like a mother dog breaking up a puppy fight. I stepped between them, lifting my elbows to look bigger and growling my disapproval in my deepest voice to say in dog talk, "Knock it off." Koda ran back over the border. Jill sidled toward the house. As she walked, her rear was toward Koda, usually an expression of the retreating coward in dog talk. Safe on her own territory, Koda barked viciously. Distance changed the meaning of that retreat. Jill ignored her and trotted along beside me, head and tail up, announcing her victory.

STRANGER TO STRANGER

When two strange dogs meet, do not know who is dominant, and therefore must find out in order to know how to relate to one another, the conversation might go something like this dog talk that I picked up on the main street of my hometown.

Two men were walking toward each other, one with a shepherd at his heels, the other a boxer. Neither dog was on a leash, but both were heeling nicely. About fifty feet from each other they broke away and rushed together. They sniffed noses. They held their tails out straight—horizontal to the ground. (This posture announces that they do not know who is boss. Watch for it and pull your dog away. It usually means that a fight to establish dominance is next.)

The owners did not seem to know what their dogs were saying, for they did not call them off. The dogs proceeded with the war talk. They presented rear ends simultaneously. (An inviolable dog law is that anus sniffing is truce time. No one attacks.) While these two gathered information about

Greeting of strangers who don't know who's boss

Truce time

The fight begins

each other, their owners came together, raised eyebrows, and simultaneously decided to leash their dogs. The shepherd's master took the leash out of his pocket, and the clip inadvertently hit the boxer in the leg. Thinking the shepherd had violated the truce and attacked him, the boxer went through the entire war vocabulary: wrinkled forehead, wrinkled nose, widened eyes emphasized further by dilated pupils, lips pulled back, two canines exposed, deep snarling growl, stiff legs. He attacked, grabbing the shepherd by the throat and twisting him to the ground. The shepherd, apparently a high-ranking dog, refused to roll onto his back in submission. He snarled as if to kill and flashed the whites of his eyes, a signal used by many mammals to admit being down but not beaten.

The masters grabbed their snarling, barking animals and pulled them apart. The shepherd was pulled into his nearby car, and the door was slammed shut. The incident seemed to be over.

The two men talked, probably about their dogs, and as they did, the boxer raised his leg and urinated on the pants cuff of the shepherd's master. Why? Was he making him familiar? Was he a new object in his environment? Or did he know what people think about such an action? Some dog talk is beyond me.

THE BULLY

There is one final dog "greeting"—a brutal one—that puts both man and beast in their place: the *humiliation*, or *bully*, *strike*. There is a human counterpart, as I learned from a young lady my mother took me to meet as a child because she had such nice manners. Mother hoped I might learn graciousness from her. The little girl came slowly down the steps of her home holding out her skirt, curtsied, and said, "I'm

Mrs. Humphrey's little daughter." Hardly had I time to be impressed when she gave me a swift kick in the shins, reducing me to scum.

In the dog version the bully rushes a rival and hits him hard with his shoulder, then twists and strikes again with his rump. The victim yelps, the bully strikes again and again, reducing the rival to a bruised and hurting omega who cringes and creeps off in disgrace. This strike is also used by some of the large herding breeds to push cattle around and by wolves to throw their prey off balance. However used, the humiliation strike is a powerful message, but dogs are more honorable than "Mrs. Humphrey's little daughter." They warn you first.

Basil, a half Lab, half poodle belonging to my friend Ellan Young, gave me the humiliation strike one day as I approached her house. Bounding toward me, tail straight out and bristling, he hit me so hard with shoulder and rump that I cried out in pain and, yes, in humiliation. I should have known—his tail had broadcast his intentions.

WATCH THAT TAIL

Ever since Basil told me off, I have learned to watch dog tails as signals of what is to come. The tail emphasizes what is going on up front. They are the ultimate semaphore. Siberian and Alaskan malamutes and the spitzes carry coiled dusters over their backs that signal over long distances. The Gordon setter slashes a baleenlike spear—slender to avoid brush and briars. The poodle sports a pompom on the end of its tail because breeders like the emphasis. And the Scottish terrier flourishes a vertical, tapered rod. Although tails are important signalers, pinschers, boxers, and those other dogs whose tails are clipped at birth do adapt to this handicap, possibly be-

THE DOG'S TAIL POSITIONS

"Who's boss?"

"I'm boss."

"I'm somebody important."

"I'm depressed."

"I'm a terrible dog."

"I'm an omega."

"I'm about to fight."

"Maybe I'll fight."

"I'm at ease, all's well."

cause the tail is only a backup system for the face. The intense messages go on up front. Nevertheless, the tail should be watched for its own sake. It says a lot.

The tail has three properties: position, shape, and movement. The message, depending on the breed, goes something like this:

Tail up and gently curved: "I'm confident."

Your answer to this is to proceed with what you are both doing. The state of affairs is good.

Tail up with a crick (a sharp bend seen particularly in wolves and shepherds): "I'm going to fight."

Remove yourself and your dog from the opponent.

A crick in the tip of the tail: "I'm threatening you, but I may not attack."

Your reply is to dominate at all costs.

Tail held straight down with hairs bristling at the tip, which is slightly raised: "I'm depressed."

An answer to this is more attention or a call to the vet. The dog could be sick.

Tail held low and brushing sideways, no raised hairs: "I'm no good. I cast myself down."

Answer this by discerning the cause. Too much pressure to perform correctly is being put upon the dog, or you may be too dominant and harsh for a particular animal. Sometimes the tail says this to another dog.

Tail straight out and all hairs bristling: "Don't come any closer. I warn you. I'll attack."

Back up, as I should have done to escape Basil the bully.

Most wonderful, the dog's tail wag is its tribute to life. The dog wags its tail only at living things. A tail wag, the equivalent of a human smile, is bestowed upon people, dogs, cats, squirrels, even mice and butterflies—but no lifeless things. A dog won't wag its tail to its dinner or to a bed, car, stick, or even a bone. The dog appreciates and responds to aliveness; it is not a materialist, and we love that quality in it. Joshua, my friend Sara Stein's child, upon noting the power of expression in his dog's tail, asked for a fake tail when he was little but mourned that he couldn't wag it and talk like a dog talks.

HOW TO TALK IN DOG POSES

To some extent, you can mimic dog body language to say some things to your pet if you loosen up enough and do not mind looking ridiculous. Get down on all fours and spank the ground to ask your dog to play, or bow slightly and slap your legs. Grasp its muzzle in your mouth to assert your leadership, or, if that seems primitive, lay your chin over its muzzle, or take its nose in your hand and shake its head gently back and forth—same message. And, if you have an omega that cowers at your step, roll on your back to say that it is no worse than you.

My son Craig used this body talk on Sadie, who belonged to his best friend, Tom Melvin. Sadie and Craig had a problem. When Craig came to visit, which was often, Sadie would cringe, roll over on her back, and, using the most self-demeaning statement in all of dogdom, urinate in that position. She retrogressed to a helpless pup.

This was, needless to say, a problem. Papers were put out and rags were made available for Sadie's greeting to Craig. Visits were curtailed. Then Craig came up with an inspiration after reading about the language of the wolves. He opened the door to Tom's house one day, called Sadie, and before she could roll over, went down on all fours and rolled onto his back, hands folded over his chest, knees pulled up. Sadie braked to a halt, sniffed Craig's face, and put a paw on his chest to ride up in dominance. Thereafter, she met him head-on with her tail and head up. The rags and newspapers were put away.

A TIME FOR LOVE

A charming characteristic of the wolves that some dogs have is the habit of bringing home presents to the family. I watched the beta wolf of Sanctuary River bring a stout white stick to the den area and drop it in the midst of the pups. They pounced on it, carried it around, and fought for it, recalling to me Sara, the dog of my children's youth.

Sara, half Lab, half Newfoundland, often came home with the kids' jackets, shoes, boots, hats, even school books that had been laid on the ground while the children played. Once, she brought home a turkey left on the neighbor's back porch by a delivery man. On my daughter Twig's fourteenth birthday, Sara stood at the door with a bouquet of asters wrapped in florist's paper. Phone calls to the neighbors and local florists turned up no owner, so we put the flowers in a vase and enjoyed the gift. To this day, my daughter insists that the quiver of celebration in the air stirred the ancient wolf-giver in Sara, and so she went out and got a present.

Siberian and Alaskan malamutes are also generous gift bringers. Qimmiq had a strong thought in his head when he bit off a small branch of rhododendron and carried it up on the porch. It lay there until I came to the door. Then he picked it up, put it in my palm, and let go, making no effort to take it back as he does with his play sticks. I had been given a present, and I thanked him with effusive palaver and a hug. To kiss him on the nose, which I do on some occasions, would have been an insult in this instance. The body language would have been pulling rank, and Qimmiq was already doing what he thought was appropriate.

A COMMON TONGUE

Finally, the dog communicates with us and its kind by voice, the medium we understand best, although it is not the dog's most expressive vehicle. The dog has five sounds: the *whimper* (also called the *whine*), the *yelp*, the *growl*, the *bark*, and, in some breeds, the *howl*.

The whimper is a group of high, plaintive cries, softly uttered, that sound pitiful and helpless. It is used by puppies to get their mother's attention and by adult dogs to get their master's attention and to beg for something they want.

When the whimper crescendoes into a sound so high-pitched and so penetrating that it seems to pierce the eardrum, it is called a whine. Sounded higher, the whine goes out of range of the human ear, and only the face and eyes reveal that anything is being said. A slight frown is visible, and the eyes are pulled down slightly at the corners to invite concern and, it is hoped, affection. Females whimper and whine more than males, for these pleas are the language of the estrous season, spoken to invite courtship. My dog Jill whimpered in the middle of the night to ask me to open the door and let her run with her lovers. She also directed her whimpers to me, saying, "I want to be your friend." The same sound is also called the social squeak; pet wolves make it to invite friendliness with people or dogs.

If you talk to your dog with the whimper, you might get a baffled look with the head tilted to one side. After all, alphas don't whimper for attention. Past that initial puzzled look, which is actually tuning in the ears better to figure out your terrible accent, you might get a tail wag for an answer. Quite often a dog will give whimpering people the "Let's-play" response, spanking the ground with the front paws, holding the rear end up.

The yelp is agony. It turns the heads of masters and dogs and needs no translation. Even a child reacts to the pain in the cry and hurries to rescue the dog. The yelp has shades of meaning depending on the age of the dog. The puppy yelp, as mentioned earlier, means surprise, hunger, pain, and cold; a yelp from an adult dog says it is injured or thinks it is about to be injured. The adult also yelps from psychological injury when given the humiliation blow.

The growl is a low, muttered complaint, and its meaning is eminently clear. Dogs growl when they are threatening one another while standing head to tail, when they warn off a stranger, when they are protecting house, den, or food, or when they want to be left alone. The deeper the growl, as with Jill and Koda, the more dominant the dog. It is an unfriendly statement.

I have only known one person who could put off a dog by using a growl. The postman who delivered our mail in Poughkeepsie, New York, could send our hound into full retreat by growling deep in his throat as he came up the walk. Yet, oddly enough, sound experts claim that the sound-wave pattern of human word whining ("Please, Mommy, pretty please") and human growling ("Get out of here!") are the same as those of dog and wolf whines and growls.

The bark of the dog is one of the least pleasant of animal vocalizations. It is monotonous and boring, a single note usually repeated over and over again to say, "Someone is approaching the house," or "Stand back, stranger," or "A dog is on our property," or just "Here I am." A professor of animal behavior at the University of Chicago counted the barks of the champion of barkers, the cocker spaniel: 907 barks in ten minutes. My uncle had a cocker that could run that dog a good second, and I am sorry to say no one was unhappy when he died.

Dogs, like wolves, have two kinds of bark. One is alarm, the other is a threat or a challenge to intruders. The alarm bark is short. The threatening or challenging bark is often several sharp barks followed by more drawn-out ones. Directed toward you, either one can be a demand to be fed or to go on an outing, depending on the circumstances.

At night the challenge bark becomes a roster. When the sounds of traffic die down and the last train has rumbled off to the city, Leon, a mutt at the bottom of the hill near the swamp, awakens and barks once. I hear him and wait. He barks again, then again; and he waits. Apparently he hears another voice that I cannot, for the next time Leon barks, he is excited. Finally I hear the distant dog, for someone has let him out. He barks, "*Bow, bow, bow*," for almost two minutes. A third dog speaks up, then far over the hill toward the next town a fourth sounds. The dogs are checking in, calling out their identities, letting each other know where they are, keeping tabs, keeping in touch—messages they can send only when the town has quieted down and all but the dogs and night animals are asleep. I find the night check-in reassuring. The dogs, by taking roll call, are saying, "All is well."

In contrast to the bark, the howl is a colorful and thrilling song. It is a gift from the wolf passed down through four thousand generations to some domestic dogs.

THE HOWL OF THE WILD

Dog howlers are the malamutes, huskies, German shepherds, and individuals of some other breeds. Some individuals howl only as pups, which suggests that the urge to howl has been weakened in breeding or that it is stifled with age. A few dogs that aren't ordinarily howlers will howl if they hear howling. When I played the phonograph record *The Language and Music of the Wolves,* sung by wolves and narrated by Robert Redford, Jill listened in great anxiety and said so by trotting restlessly around the room, whimpering, licking my hand, and trembling her jaw. Eventually she sat down, formed her mouth into an O, and howled with the wolves. As she joined the electronic chorus, she seemed to lose all contact with her human family and slip off to some distant landscape.

Scientists are still unsure why dogs howl, but just about every owner has his opinion. Ramon, a Baja fisherman, says his dog howls when he is lonely for the wilderness. Hank, an artist who lives in the next town, thinks his shepherd howls because his ears hurt when the fire whistle blares. The violin

teacher at the bottom of the hill believes his dog howls to tell a student he has hit a sour note.

A dog might howl for the same reason the wolf howls: to bind the pack together before the hunt. Wolves howl also to identify themselves to their fellows when scouting separately for food or trotting off to check a border alone. Mech's latest research indicates that the wolf pack howls to space themselves and keep distance between the packs.

Michael Fox speculates that howls, both solo and group, might be brought on by restless anxiety: The prey is not in sight, the pups are hungry, a storm is coming.

Many of us who have heard wolves howl feel it is also a celebration. The music is rollicking, at times jubilant, and the tails wag joyfully.

The group howl, like our musical events, has form. The sing-along is generally initiated by the alpha male wolf with a series of short tuneful notes. The second wolf, either the beta male or the alpha female, comes in with a solo, the others join one at a time, then all howl in unison, in expectation, in magic. The howls start low and work up to shorter and higher notes that break into barks and end abruptly when the breath is used up.

Wolves appreciate people joining their choruses, but they have to obey their rules. Each wolf wants its own note. Anyone who joins in must harmonize. When Mech was howling with the wolves of Ely one moonlit night, he howled the same note as one of the pack. The wolf stopped, listened to Mech's note, then politely took another.

In questioning the experts about the meaning of howling, it was Gordon Haber who put it most succinctly: "It's fun." And it is. Upon the conclusion of a wolf-cry musical composition at the Kennedy Center for the Performing Arts in 1979, composer-conductor Paul Winter turned to the audience. "And now," he said, lifting his baton, "let's all howl. It is wonderful to do." We threw back our heads, rounded our mouths, and, closing our eyes, howled as if we had finally found the joyful road to the center of the universe.

PLAIN ENGLISH

Mostly, dogs are very much in our world. Another "How-does-my-dog-know-when-I-am-going-out?" story makes the point. The clue that Groschen, a German shepherd, used baffled her master for years.

"I would be sitting at the breakfast table with my wife, still drinking my coffee and talking about my plans," my friend Dave Pollack told me, "when suddenly Groschen would get up and go to the door. I was going to drive to town, and she knew it, although I never made a move.

"For years I experimented with all the gimmicks that might have tipped her off. I jangled the car keys, put on my coat, took out my wallet when I was not going to town. But I didn't fool her; she didn't go to the door.

"One day my wife was sick. I carried a cup of coffee upstairs to her. The dog was sleeping on the floor beside the bed.

" 'I'm going to town,' I said, as I always do before departing. 'What do you need?'

"Groschen walked out of the room and went downstairs to the door.

" 'She understands English!' I exclaimed.

"My wife looked at me in disgust.

" 'Of course, she does! What do you think she understands—German?' "

Dogs do learn our language. When my son and I were in Baja, Mexico, he called, "Here, doggie!" to a black-and-white dog trotting across the street of Cabo San Lucas. The dog trotted on.

"Perro, aquí!" he tried. Instantly the little dog turned around and came running up to him. The message was not in the tone of Craig's voice or in his body language. The dog knew Spanish.

Dogs are much better at learning our language than we are at learning theirs. Statements like "Let's go for a walk" are understood by most dogs even when said casually. A neighbor of mine looks at her dog around nine o'clock in the evening and says, "Shanty, it's time to go to bed." The bright-eyed mutt looks up at her, arises, and trots off to the cellar where his bed is laid.

And that smart Nele goes into conniptions when someone mentions the word "cookie." The family has been forced to spell out the word to prevent Nele from barging into the kitchen and making a scene.

One friend counted twenty-seven words that his dog knew and responded to, "and many more," he added, "when you consider that I put those key words in phrases."

A dog is more than man's best friend and more than a faithful Old Dog Tray. The very nature of its sensory system, its feelings for family, and its love of life make it, for better or for worse, like a good, loving partner in marriage. After a few years of talking and gesturing to your dog, the two of you come into exquisite communication, as in those close marriages in which the spouses know each other so well that their anticipation of one another's meanings is the closest thing we know to mind reading. Qimmiq need not whine for a biscuit anymore—he glances from me to the closet where I keep them. "Okay," I say, open the door, and pick one up. Sometimes I say nothing, just act. In the woods I need not ask him to sit when we come to the top of the hill in view of the glorious Hudson. He glances at me, then the vista, sits down, and, like myself, gazes across the river valley.

Only a few weeks ago we were on a new trail that opened up over a lake. Qimmiq glanced back at me, ran to the ridge, and sat down. "You're right, it is beautiful," I said. He wagged his tail. His wild kin, the wolves of Mount McKinley, dig their dens high on hills in view of gray-green valleys and snow-covered peaks. And they, like Qimmiq and me, sit and enjoy the magnificence. At such moments a glance from either of us will say a volume, and the abyss between species is crossed from both sides.

But the course of talking to your dog does not always run that smoothly.

I was panting to Qimmiq, asking him in his own language to play with me, but he did not respond. I was persistent—hanging out my tongue, hyperventilating and dreaming as I did so of that different land from which he had come, the Arctic. It is a land of the northern lights, where the moon sets and rises an hour later, of sun dogs and ice fog, of hoarfrost and no rats, mice, cockroaches, or fleas. Carried away by my daydreams, I spoke in my own tongue.

"And so, beautiful dog," said I out loud, "is it that land that makes you so noble? Is it that sky that makes you so beautiful?"

He frowned and, wishing to please, went upstairs and brought down my sneaker.

Closer Than We Thought

At a barbecue in the suburbs of Athens, Georgia, I found myself seated on a spacious wooden deck among a group of psychologists and anthropologists, professors and their graduate students. As the night crossed over into morning, the philosopher in each emerged and the truth of yesterday became today's error.

We were discussing animal behavior as a route toward understanding nonhuman communication, and the conversation had been meandering like an old river.

"The first thing we have to do," said an authoritative voice to my left, "is to settle what the difference is between man and the animals so that we know who we are and who they are."

I searched my memory, recalling that when I was in college the word was that the difference between man and beast was our ability to make and use tools. We throw stones, spear food on forks, and carry things in jars and baskets. These achievements, experts believed then, were unique to *Homo sapiens,* and textbooks referred to our species as the *tool user.* That was the late 1930s and early 1940s.

I certainly was not going to mention this long-disproved notion to the esteemed researchers around me, some of whom had just heard the latest in nonhuman tool use from chimpanzee watcher Jane Goodall. While traveling in Serengeti National Park in northern Tanzania, she and her husband, Hugo van Lawick, brought their car to a sudden halt in an open savanna where two Egyptian vultures—white birds with golden cheeks and about the size of ravens—were standing before an ostrich egg. One of the birds had a stone in its beak. It threw back its head, flipped its neck forward, and hurled the stone. It struck the huge thick-shelled egg with a thud. The vulture walked up to the egg, saw that it had not broken, and, doing some obvious thinking, picked up the stone for another try. The next pitch missed the egg entirely, but with the third effort the shell cracked, and it took only a few more hurls to open it.

Sea otters also use stones as hammers. They collect large hard-shelled abalones in their teeth during dives to the sea bottom, then each picks up a stone with its forepaws. Surfacing, the otters roll onto their backs, place the abalones on their bellies, and, clasping a stone in both front feet, smash the shells open.

One of the Galápagos Islands finches uses a cactus spine or a sharp twig as a fork. First, it tests the tool's strength by pressing it against a limb. If it breaks, it seeks a stronger one. Then the bird transfers it to a foot while it uses its beak to drill into the wood of a decaying tree. When an insect is found, the finch takes the spine in its beak again and guides it into the hole. With precision it spears the insect and pulls it out. Shifting the spine to its foot, the bird then eats its meal from the pick.

Jane Goodall was the first to report that at least some animals—the chimpanzees she was observing at Gombe Game Preserve—make the tools they use. To get drinking water trapped in tree cavities, chimpanzees crumple leaves to make a sponge. They "fish" for termites with a probe they fashion by carefully stripping the leaves from a slender branch. The probe is stuck into the termite corridor. Considering themselves invaded, the termites grab the foreign intruder in their jaws and hang on while the chimp pulls them out and eats them like shish kebab.

Impressive as these technologies are, it could be argued that they are instinctive, programmed behavior not comparable to the thoughtful way even a toddler might use a stone one time to crush a peanut, another time to scratch a table, and still another to bang against a pot. That's what I had thought, until Crowbar, our pet crow, taught me a lesson.

Crowbar, who enjoyed playing with my children, was in the sandbox with them one morning. Presently my daughter came running to tell me she did not want to play with Crowbar anymore because he did not play fair. He took all the toys and hoarded them in the crotches of the apple tree. I suggested she slide down the slide.

"Crows can't slide," I explained of my plot to foil the bird. "The bottoms of their feet are horny to keep them from slipping off tree limbs. Crowbar will stick at the top."

Fifteen minutes later I looked out to see my daughter and son sliding down the slide and Crowbar at the top— stuck. He was forced to hop down. I felt smug about having outwitted a crow.

A moment later, Crowbar was back in the sandbox. There he picked up a plastic coffee-can lid, flew with it to the top of the slide, put it down, stepped in it, and—zoom.

The young woman sitting next to me at the barbecue apparently had been mentally going over similar territory. Perhaps, she wondered aloud, an individual animal's failure to pass creative invention along to others marks the boundary between human and nonhuman. No sooner were the words out of her mouth than she retracted them. She had remembered the macaques that have been protected for generations at the Monkey Research Center, Takasakiyama, Japan. For years the monkeys had accepted wheat, soybeans, and sweet potatoes tossed on the ground to supplement the foods they could forage for themselves. These treats, though eagerly sought, were unpleasantly gritty.

In a moment of thoughtful inspiration, a young female monkey scooped up a handful of food and ran to the stream. Seating herself beside a pool, she dumped her sandy ration into the water. The dirt sank to the bottom, the food floated to the surface, and she scooped up the clean morsels and ate them grit-free.

Her mother and siblings observed, understood what she was doing, and learned to wash grain, too.

Ultimately, the food-washing invention was taken up by the younger set. Conservative elders never did go for the new fad, but by the following generation, most had adopted food washing. It had become a tradition.

If that was not sufficiently startling—primates are certainly smart, after all—the spread of an invention among a group of birds in England was enough to make the hair stand on end.

Blue tits, little birds like our chickadees, learned to flip the lids off milk bottles and sip cream during World War II in the village of Swathling, England. The lid-flipping technique spread from a few birds to almost the entire town population of tits and, a year later, to populations in towns ten miles away. The milk industry answered complaints by urging customers to put stones on their porches to be placed on top of the bottles by the milk deliverers. The stones were put out, but customers found them beside, not on top of, the bottles in the morning. More calls to the milk company. Officials insisted the deliverers had put the stones on the bottles. One suspicious housewife got up before dawn and peeked out from behind the blind to see if this were the case. It was true. The deliverer had dutifully placed a stone on each bottle. She was perplexed. Then came the blue tits. Without hesitation they alighted on the stones and pecked at their edges until they shifted over and toppled to the ground. With a whack the pretty blue-and-gold birds flipped the cardboard lids and sipped cream.

The next ploy was to cover the bottles with towels. This halted the assault on the cream for several days, and then towels were found cast aside, and cream sipping resumed. A check at dawn revealed that birds in groups of three or four each took a corner of the towel, lifted it off the bottles while flying, and dropped it; then they flitted back to the bottles, flipped the lids, and sipped.

Diabolically, the milk deliverers placed the morning's delivery in a box open on one side, but barely taller than a milk bottle so that there was no clearance for the birds. This briefly foiled the blue tits, which were now accustomed to matching their wits with humans'.

But before long the blue tits, now on their mental toes, simply flew into the open-backed milk trucks while the milkmen shoved bottles into the box on the stoop, and sipped cream there.

My mind drifted on the wings of birds as the balmy night drew on and the conversation flowed—I was remembering a chicken.

Her name was Helen, and she belonged to my childhood

friend Virginia. She was one of those Easter gifts who grew from a cute fuzzy plaything into a serious personality. Helen was much more than a hen. She not only followed my friend but called her to meals by clucking furiously if Virginia did not hear her mother's dinner call. She conveniently laid an egg a day on a towel in the corner near the kitchen stove. She made a hobby of carrying pebbles from one bowl to another, for no apparent reason but that it amused everyone, not least herself. When Virginia and I played jump rope, Helen flew back and forth over the low swinging rope, clucking and carrying on in her "Look-what-I-did" egg-laying voice.

Then there was Sam. I would never have believed in Sam had I not met a professional naturalist who knew him and Peter, a boy of ten, and reported her observations to me. Sam was Peter's box turtle.

"Do you love me, Sam?" the boy asked as he gently held him against his throat beneath his chin. Slowly Sam opened his box, slowly extended his head and neck, and moved them gently back and forth against Peter's throat.

"He's saying 'I love you,' " Peter explained.

"Tell me you love me good," he insisted and tipped his chin against Sam. The turtle stroked Peter again.

"Let's go for a walk, Sam," Peter said, and slowly Sam pulled into his shell. Peter put him in his pocket and strode out the door and down the path.

I thought of all manner of scientific explanations for Sam's behavior: that the warmth of the boy's skin had made the turtle stretch his neck; that the pressure on his shell had provoked him to—something. But Peter's mother reported this:

"Sam sleeps with Peter—right on his chest."

"Of course Peter puts him there?"

"Oh, no. Sam climbs up the tumbled blankets when

Peter is asleep, walks onto his chest, and stops. He pulls his head and neck into his box. I presume he's sleeping too. He's very quiet."

Could it be that animals so different from ourselves can be brought out of their faraway worlds into communication with humans?

"Well, one thing is certain," a voice interrupted my musings. "We can't say that the difference between man and nonhuman animals is that only we use language."

"That's still controversial," said a graduate student in psychology whose mentor was one of the firm believers that animals cannot use language.

Most linguists concur that two criteria must be met for a system of communication to constitute a language. One is that the words or signs be symbols for something and recognized as such by the user. That may or may not be a reasonable demand. Jean Piaget, the Swiss psychologist who did more to unravel the thought processes of children than perhaps anyone, discovered that to a three-year-old, words are the objects they stand for. They use symbols without knowing that they do.

The other criterion for a communication system to be a language is that the symbols be combinable with one another to form novel phrases or sentences that are nonetheless understandable by others. Any three-year-old can do that.

Research efforts to resolve the question of whether or not animals could use language foundered for a while on the fact that even our closest relative, the chimpanzee, hasn't the vocal apparatus to speak. Chimps raised like babies within a human family had learned to grunt a few words like "cup" or "milk," but no more.

Then, in the late 1960s, psychologists began to circumvent that obstacle by using nonvocal languages. David Premack of the University of California at Santa Barbara used plastic symbols of different shapes to represent words. He claimed that chimp Sarah learned some 130 words and phrases with this technique, but admitted that she had created nothing new to say.

Psychologists Allen and Beatrice Gardner of the University of Nevada fueled the debate when they taught the chimp Washoe to communicate with humans in American Sign Language (Ameslan), a gestural language used by the deaf. Washoe astounded scientist and layman alike not only by learning 125 signs but by inventing a novel phrase of her own. One day, seeing a swan swimming on a lake, but not knowing the sign for it, Washoe excitedly signed out "water bird."

Skeptics Dr. Duane Rumbaugh of Georgia State University and his wife, Susan Savage Rumbaugh, suggested that the people who were teaching the chimps these novel nonvocal languages were so involved with the animals that they were suffering from the Clever Hans effect. Clever Hans, a horse who lived around the turn of the century, was credited for a time with being able to solve arithmetic problems. When shown an addition or subtraction problem written on a blackboard, he would stamp out the correct answer with his hoof. Close study showed that Clever Hans did not know the answers. Instead he was picking up subtle clues from his trainer, who was unaware himself of what he was doing, that told the horse when to start and when to stop stamping.

This made skeptics of almost all animal behaviorists for the next forty years.

To offset the possibility that researchers were unconsciously cueing their students, Rumbaugh invented a language based on ancient Chinese, dubbed it *Yerkish,* reduced the words to lexigrams, or symbols, and programmed them into a computer at the Yerkes Primate Research Center in Atlanta. A special keyboard using the Yerkish lexigrams was designed, and the computer was connected to various appurtenances, such as a vending machine and a movie projector. In order to obtain, say, a candy, the chimp would have to ask for it in a certain way: "Please, machine, give [name of chimp] candy." Each word was a symbol over a button, and correctly stated requests were answered automatically. A bright young chimp named Lana was domiciled in a playroom fitted to a chimp's taste with swings, windows, ledges—and the computer. After a few demonstrations, Lana was adroitly pushing the correct lexigrams in the correct syntax to obtain all her needs: water, food, candy, movies of chimps. By pushing the right buttons she could call Tim, a graduate student and her human friend, to come play with her and relieve her boredom with the machine.

Lana toppled mankind's superiority complex when she not only learned which buttons to push to get what she wanted but forced her human friends to create new lexigrams for items that had not originally been programmed into the machine. One day she taught Tim to tickle her, a favorite chimpanzee pleasure, and then got the idea across to put the word "tickle" on the machine. After that, she could push the buttons to say, "Please, Tim, come tickle Lana." Over the years she learned 125 word-symbols, developed counting skills, and compared piles of objects to say which had the greater number.

"Twenty years ago," said Rumbaugh in the winter of 1984, "if you had told me that apes could learn words in a meaningful way, I and other scientists would have said, 'That's impossible.' Now that's no longer a question. The answer is yes, they do."

The naysaying graduate student was upholding the opposition. He referred to the work of psychologist Herbert Terrace of Columbia University and his little chimp Nim (full name Nim Chimpsky, a play on the name of linguist Noam Chomsky of M.I.T., a proponent of the idea that language ability is biologically unique to humans). Terrace and his students put Nim through forty-four months of intensive sign-language drill while treating him much as they would a child. He learned aptly, signing "dirty" when he wanted to use the potty or "drink" when he spotted someone sipping from a thermos. Nim, said Terrace, nonetheless did not master even the rudiments of grammar or sentence construction. Unlike children, his speech did not grow in complexity, nor did it show much spontaneity. Eighty-eight percent of the time, he "talked" only in response to questions from his teachers. Terrace studied the tapes of other apes and concluded, "The closer I looked, the more I regarded the many reported instances of language as elaborate tricks (by the apes) for obtaining rewards."

If so, an ape had certainly fooled me. I had visited the famous Lana in the company of Dr. Rumbaugh to see this wunderkind for myself. As we approached the two-way glass side of her playroom, the alert chimp turned, saw me with her friend, and began to show off. She swung down to her machine, which glowed with symbols for some fifty words at that time, and smiled a toothy chimpanzee smile. The symbols on the keyboard had translations behind the scenes for the professors and assistants, who could not remember them all.

Glancing at me once again, she began typing, moving her hands so rapidly that I could barely follow the sequence of buttons she pushed.

"Please, machine." She pushed two of the lexigrams. "Give Lana M & M's." Three more buttons were pushed. Tim, who had been taking notes behind a one-way window where Lana couldn't see him, suddenly stood up. Lana was looking at the "water" button. She wanted M & M's *and* water. She needed a new word. She needed "and" right then and there to circumvent the long procedure of pushing two full sentences of lexigrams.

"That's when the machine seems frustrating," Tim said to me later. "I can't give her the new word she wants fast enough. She thinks faster than we can work."

"I think it's a matter of cultivating a process that's inherent in chimps," Dr. Rumbaugh explained to me. "They can symbolize. They can learn; absolutely they can learn."

Dr. Rumbaugh knows, as every pet owner knows, that the more you talk to an animal, whether in its language or ours, the smarter and more aware it becomes.

"Language changes and enhances chimps' lives," he said. "The language-smart chimps are much more reflective and communicative. They interrelate with humans differently and more effectively and are more clever in learning and solving problems. Even their demeanor is changed. They are less destructive and much more careful in their interacting with people."

There is not an animal owner who would not agree. The cats, dogs, birds, and horses—even wild creatures that have been brought into a dialogue with humans—seem to grow more clever, considerate, and aware. They are more careful of us.

Or is it the other way around? It seemed to me, watching Lana spell out her wishes to "machine," that opening up an avenue of communication between our two separate species had increased our awareness, sensitivity, and intelligence as much as it had the chimps'. Perhaps we are becoming clever enough to see just how clever they have always been.

As I left the incredible Lana to manipulate her human friends with her machine, Tim accompanied me.

"At long last," he said enthusiastically, "we are beginning to talk to the animals. Soon I will be able to ask Lana the sixty-four-dollar question."

"And what is that?" I asked.

"What do you think of people?"

That question may have been answered by Koko, a hulking female gorilla taught sign language by Francine Patterson, a psychologist at Stanford University.

Koko has made her human companions aware not only that her breed is bright, but that it shares devious abilities commonly held to be unique to people.

Koko can lie, argue, and insult.

Writes Patterson:

At six o'clock on a spring evening, I went to the trailer where Koko lives to put her to bed. I was greeted by Cathy Ransom, one of my assistants, who told me she and Koko had been arguing. The dispute began when Koko was shown a poster of herself. Using hands and fingers, Cathy had asked Koko, "What's this?"

"Gorilla," signed Koko.

"Who gorilla?" asked Cathy.

"Bird," responded bratty Koko, and things went downhill from there.

"You bird?" asked Cathy.

"You," countered Koko.

"Not me. You are bird," rejoined Cathy, mindful that "bird" can be an insult in Koko's lexicon.

"Me gorilla," asserted Koko.

"Who bird?" asked Cathy.

"You nut," signed Koko.

"You nut, not me," Cathy replied.

Finally, Koko gave up. Plaintively she signed, "Damn, me good," and walked away.

"What makes all this awesome," continues Patterson, "is that Koko, by all accepted concepts of animal and human nature, should not be able to do any of this. Traditionally, such behavior has been considered uniquely human; yet here is a language-using gorilla."

Koko can get into contrary moods, once considered the prerogative of humans. Patterson can almost program her actions when she is in such a mood. When she was breaking plastic spoons, an assistant signed, "Good, break them," and instantly Koko stopped breaking them and started kissing them. She knows she is misbehaving on these occasions and once described herself as a "stubborn devil."

Koko has a rich collection of insults that she has invented—"rotten stink" and "dirty toilet," as well as "bird" and "nut." These she applies to people whom she is not getting along with. During a fit of pique she referred to Patterson, whom she calls Penny, as "Penny toilet dirty devil"—a real achievement in creativity in any language.

Koko creates not only novel phrases and meanings but new symbols. She is terrified of alligators, although she has never seen a real one, just toothy facsimiles. For signing about them, she has invented her own word by snapping the two palms together in an imitation of an alligator's jaws closing. "Large alligator" is a big movement with her arms; "little alligator" is a tiny movement with her fingers.

Koko can refer to events removed in time and space, a sophisticated characteristic of human language known to linguists as *displacement*.

Patterson: "What did you do to Penny?"

Koko: "Bite." (The bite, which had occurred three days earlier, had been called a scratch by Koko at the time.)

Patterson: "You admit it?"

Koko: "Sorry bite scratch."

Patterson: "Why bite?"

Koko: "Because mad."

Patterson: "Why mad?"

Koko: "Don't know."

But was Koko really ignorant of her motive? A wonderful thing about language is that it can be used to deceive as well as inform, to evade as well as confront.

It was during a confrontation with a reporter that Koko might indirectly have answered the question, What do you think of people? The reporter wanted to know whether Koko, who had been raised among people her whole life, thought of herself as a fellow human. Translating, Patterson signed: "Are you an animal or a person?" Instantly came Koko's response: "Fine animal gorilla."

Until recently animal-speech teachers thought language had to be taught by humans to each individual primate and could not be passed on to other members of the species.

Again the animals proved us wrong. All the chimpanzees that learned sign and symbol language are now teaching their knowledge to offspring and to untutored adult chimps. All are conversing.

The conversation at the barbecue heated into an argument as to whether or not the chimps and Koko know what they are saying, and promptly stalemated. The question pivots on the word "know," for if Koko knows she is a "fine animal gorilla," then she is conscious, aware of herself and of her thoughts. Consciousness, particularly self-consciousness, has become the last bastion for those who would protect our uniqueness among animals.

All other differences have scattered like duckpins under strike after strike of facts.

Our esthetic sense?

The male bowerbird is an artist. With a sense of design he skillfully decorates his love arbor with colorful petals, berries, and "found" objects to please the critic—the female. Certain colors are more favored than others, and each ornament is placed to emphasize its position within an overall design. Moreover, one species of this bird, the regent bowerbird, paints with a brush and pigment. He mixes earth colors, plant pigments, and charcoal with saliva, dips a wadded leaf or piece of bark in the paint, and daubs the walls of the bower he has built. The results are murals of passionate gray-blue or green.

Our ability to plan, to imagine a future event?

The alpha male wolf can figure out a strategy for attacking prey and, what is more, communicate the plan to his hunters.

Wage war? Commit murder?

There are those who find our violence and inhumanity toward man the blatant difference between us and the animals. But chimps in the Gombe Game Preserve wage war on neighboring groups that infringe on their territory, and they kill members of their own group for motives no easier to discern than "senseless" human murders.

"Our knowledge of death," a young woman had concluded earlier in the evening.

"No," I spoke up.

I had heard a Pulitzer Prize–winning scientist speak to this difference one night in Arizona, stating that the knowledge of death was the important difference between man and beast.

But had he ever seen a crow find a dead companion and bell out the death knell? Had he ever seen a crow die of strychnine-poisoned grain and then heard the flock mournfully announce the death? And did the speaker know that the crows, seeing such a disaster, learn which corn is poisoned and tell their offspring and friends?

The question of consciousness is less easily laid to rest. Crows may fear poison as wolves fear hunters, and both may connect such dangers to the sense of loss death arouses in humans too. But do they think, I, too, will die? Or do even uncannily "human" responses like Koko's self-identification as a "fine animal gorilla" represent merely mechanical learning? She might, after all, have been showing no more comprehension of her words than a child who has been taught to recite the alphabet, but who is unaware of what the letters stand for or that they can be spelled into meanings.

The discussion on that suburban deck ended around three o'clock when the moon was setting behind the pines. As we arose to leave, I felt unsatisfied. After hours of hashing and rehashing we had not concluded anything. I approached our host, the most venerable and renowned member of that late-night group of philosophers.

"So what does it all mean?" I asked.

"That we are closer to the animals than we think," came the answer.

As I stepped down from the deck, I felt I was stepping down from a tower we had mistakenly built to keep us above all other animals. I felt my kinship with the singing bird, the howling wolf, the blowing horse, and the head-bumping cat. I could see myself in them and was amused as well as impressed. I went to my room thinking of old Will Cramer. It had seemed to me, when I began to research the how-to of talking to animals, that the Will Cramers of this world would supply the magic—the intuition that, as he had told me, was "beyond words"—and that scientists would supply the hard facts. Now I realized that was not quite the case. For all their careful study, researchers eventually come face-to-face with communication that is beyond words, and for all their innocence, gifted laymen eventually uncover undeniable facts.

27 million Americans can't read a bedtime story to a child.

It's because 27 million adults in this country simply can't read.

Functional illiteracy has reached one out of five Americans. It robs them of even the simplest of human pleasures, like reading a fairy tale to a child.

You can change all this by joining the fight against illiteracy.

Call the Coalition for Literacy at toll-free **1-800-228-8813** and volunteer.

Volunteer Against Illiteracy. The only degree you need is a degree of caring.

Ad Council Coalition for Literacy

Warner Books is proud to be an active supporter of the Coalition for Literacy.